Windows on the World
from the Word

Windows *on the* World
from the Word

Ian Coffey with Kim Bush

Text copyright © Ian Coffey and Kim Bush 2001
The authors assert the moral right
to be identified as the authors of this work

Published by
Bible Reading Fellowship
First Floor, Elsfield Hall,
15–17 Elsfield Way, Oxford OX2 8EP
ISBN 1 84101 149 5

First published 2001
10 9 8 7 6 5 4 3 2 1

Acknowledgments
Unless otherwise stated, scripture quotations are taken from the *Holy Bible,*
New International Version, copyright © 1973, 1978, 1984 by International
Bible Society, are used by permission of Hodder & Stoughton Limited.
All rights reserved. 'NIV' is a registered trademark of International Bible
Society. UK trademark number 1448790.

Scriptures quoted from the Good News Bible published by The Bible
Societies/HarperCollins Publishers Ltd, UK © American Bible Society 1966,
1971, 1976, 1992, used with permission.

A catalogue record for this book is available from the British Library

Printed and bound in Great Britain by
Bookmarque, Croydon

Contents

Windows on Church

Windows on Wisdom

Windows on Family

Windows on People

Windows on the Beatitudes

Windows on Following Christ

Windows on Pain

Windows on Heaven

Introduction

This book has travelled an interesting journey.

It began in 1994 when Ian Coffey was asked by the Editor of the Western Morning News to write a weekly column giving a religious comment on the news. The first sections in the chapters of this book are made up from selections of these 'thoughts for the week'.

The 'Ian Coffey Column' has prompted a steady stream of letters from the West Country and much farther afield, as people sought permission to quote, reproduce or use the articles in a variety of ways. With these letters came suggestions for the columns to be reproduced in book form. Kim Bush has carefully worked through a selection of the articles, adding relevant readings, meditations and prayers, grouping them into sections with a common theme.

The chapters can be used on a daily, weekly or occasional basis. The themed sections provide relevant readings and comments for a variety of occasions. Topics covered include family relationships, looking at life with eyes of faith, seasons of the year and facing testing times.

Some of the opening articles in each chapter are linked to a specific news event. This reflects the fact that the articles first appeared as a newspaper column dealing with a story that was the focus of media attention at the time. Where appropriate, a note is given linking the opening article to the news event that prompted it. They offer one perspective on what it means to 'think Christianly' about national and international events and illustrate the adage that 'a Christian should read the Bible in one hand and the newspaper in the other'.

The overall aim of this book is to provide 'God thoughts' on issues in today's world. They offer windows on the world from the Word.

Ian Coffey and Kim Bush

Windows on the Year

Where did you leave your sins?

Therefore, if anyone is in Christ, he is a new creation; the old has gone, the new has come!
2 CORINTHIANS 5:17

A Dutch friend recently told me of a family tradition shared each New Year's Eve. As the midnight celebrations approached, at a given point their father would sit everyone down. The children would be invited to own up to anything they had done in the past year that had gone undiscovered. They could do so without any fear of punishment either then or in the future. My friend told me how wonderful it felt being able to confess to having broken the rules, knowing that their parents would do nothing about it!

As a parent myself, I am amazed at both the restraint and the wisdom behind such a custom and a fine example of teaching children the principle of forgiveness.

So many of us are weighed down with the baggage of guilt that an occasional amnesty would come as a great relief.

That is why the Bible continually reminds us of the value of keeping short accounts by not letting a day end when you are still out of sorts with someone, by settling matters before they escalate and, most important of all, by making our peace with our Maker before we go to meet him.

God has provided a means of forgiveness and a mechanism for finding it.

The means is through the death and resurrection of Jesus Christ on our behalf and the mechanism is through a determined willingness on our part to break with the past and travel in new directions. But this is no 'easy believism' as parodied in the phrase, 'Christians go to church on Sunday to confess all the sins committed on Saturday that they will repeat on Monday'.

New Testament Christianity demands evidence that saying sorry means a changed lifestyle. 'If anyone is in Christ, he is a new creation; the old has gone, the new has come!'

The story is told of an absent-minded woman who used to write out her list of shortcomings before going to confession each week. One day, running late and in a fluster, she popped into the supermarket on her way to church, leaving her shopping list for a helpful assistant to sort out.

On arriving at confession she proceeded to read out, 'Six pork chops, 4lb of carrots, tin of peas', before exclaiming in alarm, 'Oh, no! I've left my sins at Sainsburys!'

The truth is, as one year ends and another begins, we can leave our sins somewhere much more permanent and effective.

For further reading

PSALM 103:1–22

When we become Christians, God is aware of all our sins, including those we have forgotten and those we would rather forget. Not only that, he knows all those sins that we are going to commit. He accepts us, knowing already the worst that will ever be true of us. Sometimes, especially if we have been Christians for a long time, we do something of which we are so ashamed that we wonder how God could ever forgive us. We may try to avoid God because we feel that we cannot face him with what we have done. But God is not surprised and he doesn't change his mind about us. David says, 'He does not treat us as our sins deserve or repay us according to our iniquities' (v. 10). He has compassion on us. The first place we should go when we have sinned is to our loving Father God, and as quickly as possible.

Prayer

You, Lord, are 'compassionate and gracious, slow to anger, abounding in love' to me, undeserving as I am, and I worship you.

Everyday resolutions

And he died for all, that those who live should no longer live for themselves but for him who died for them and was raised again.
2 CORINTHIANS 5:15

Admiral Sir James Lawry Gregory had a distinguished career in the Royal Navy. He was renowned for running a tight ship and appeared to have no weaknesses of character. But there was one particularly strange thing about him. Every morning, straight after breakfast, he would retire to his cabin, open a locked box and take out a piece of paper. He would study it for a few moments before returning it and locking the box. His routine never wavered, prompting much speculation. What was written on the paper? Some verses from the Bible? A letter from his father? Some words of wisdom given at the start of his career? As the years passed, the mystery grew and so did the legend.

One day Gregory was midway through his reading ritual when he was urgently summoned to the bridge. Two junior officers seized their opportunity and slid into his cabin to read the mystery contents of the scrap of paper the Admiral studied each day. It simply read, 'Starboard on the right, port on the left.'

We all suffer (to one degree or another) from memory loss and, like Sir James, we look for ways to keep ourselves on track. I half wonder if that is where the idea of New Year resolutions comes from. January 1st is a new page, a fresh start, and we want to set out our goals for the year, whether it's losing weight or saving money—we want to get better.

The truth is, we don't have to wait until New Year's Day to make such changes. That option is available every day of the year. But the story of Gregory's little list is a helpful reminder that we too need such helpful reminders to keep us going in the right direction!

King David wrote many psalms in the Bible. One of them includes this phrase of faith: 'I trust in you, O Lord; I say, "You are my God." My times are in your hands' (Psalm 31:14–15). If you read the rest of the psalm, you will see that David did not write it at an easy time in his life, when all was going well. He uses words such as 'distress', 'sorrow', 'anguish', 'grief' and 'affliction'—all of which indicate the pressures he felt. But in the middle of such personal turmoil he found an anchoring point in his relationship with a God who never changes.

I wish you a very happy new year. And as we set sail into this new year, perhaps we all need to take a leaf out of the Admiral's book and remind ourselves every day of the little big things that are so important.

For further reading

2 CORINTHIANS 5:11—6:2

For many of us, the new year feels like a fresh start and a good time to resolve to improve on the mistakes made in the year just gone. In reality, though, it usually isn't long before we find ourselves slipping back into bad habits because, in effect, nothing has changed but the date. The only effective way to change is to 'be reconciled to God' (v. 26) so that 'we might become the righteousness of God' (v. 20). When we trust Jesus as our Saviour, God no longer counts our sins against us and we begin to live a new life not in our own strength but in his. When we make mistakes, when we sin, his forgiveness is freely available to us and we can start afresh. It's often helpful to use the new year as a time for re-evaluating how we are living, and deciding to do things differently, but unless we seek God's renewing power throughout the year, resolving daily to follow him, we are going to begin the new year no better than we began the last.

Prayer

In you, Lord, I am 'a new creation'. Thank you for the opportunity you give to make a fresh start, free from the weight of sin and guilt. Help me to grow in my faith through this new year.

Keeping in touch

Delight yourself in the Lord and he will give you the desires of your heart.

PSALM 37:4

I spent the whole of January on sabbatical, finishing a writing project. I took the opportunity to go abroad for a week, mainly for a change of scenery and to keep myself sane. Writing, particularly the academic sort, can be a lonely and tedious slog. Very few people knew where I was, so it was a shock to answer the phone one afternoon and hear my eldest son's voice.

I instantly switched into parent mode. 'If he is making an international call during the day it must be (a) a family emergency such as death or sudden illness; (b) he has been arrested and I am his one permitted phone call; (c) he has failed all his exams and is being sent home from university; or (d) he is out of cash and facing immediate financial embarrassment with the Gas Company.'

My brain swiftly calculated the possibilities and, in a split second, settled on (d), mainly because (a) to (c) have never happened before, whereas good old (d) often rears its familiar head in conversations. (Aren't children wonderful?)

The conversation continued for several minutes—about me and my thesis; about the pain of computers; about him and his exams; about books; about life. I was waiting for the punch, but it never came. He was winding down to a goodbye and the suspense was killing me. 'Great to hear from you. Why did you call?' (Liar. What I really meant was, 'What do you want?')

Then it came. The killer punch out of nowhere. Two weeks later and I am still reeling and just the retelling makes me fill up.

'Nothing really, Dad. Just wanted to see how you are and how the writing is going.'

That comment made my month. I live with the conviction that most people only want me for what I can do for them, as opposed to wanting me for who I am. One phone call brought a moment of relief to my perpetual cynicism.

More than that, I think I learned a profound lesson about prayer. I am a self-confessed failure at prayer, who just can't give up struggling to get it right. Usually I pray because I have to, prompted by some need in my life or someone else's.

But how often do I talk to God for no other reason than simply to build a relationship?

Quite a thought—for Valentine's Day.

For further reading

PSALM 145:1–21

In our busy lives, we need diaries to keep track of where we should be and when, and spend lots of time just rushing to get there. But the key to building any relationship is pausing in our busy schedules and spending time on it. King David walked closely with God and spent time with him 'every day'. In this psalm we see that he praised God, he meditated on his works and he talked to other people about him. He knew God's nature well: 'The Lord is gracious and compassionate, slow to anger and rich in love… faithful to all his promises and loving towards all he has made (vv. 8, 13). These are the kind of things he could only know from first-hand experience. Bad habits are hard to get out of, but good habits are well worth getting into, like the habit of spending time with God.

Prayer

I will exalt you, my God the King;
I will praise your name for ever and ever.
Every day I will praise you
and extol your name for ever and ever (v. 1).

Lifeboats and wheelbarrows

So the soldiers cut the ropes that held the lifeboat and let it fall away.

ACTS 27:32

There's a story told of the French tightrope walker, Blondin. In 1859 he walked a high wire 1,100 feet long, stretched 160 feet above the waters of Niagara Falls. He crossed the Falls on other occasions, with theatrical variations: blindfolded, in a sack, trundling a wheelbarrow, on stilts, carrying a man on his back and, my personal favourite, sitting down midway to make and eat an omelette!

On one of these occasions, the celebrity was interviewed by the press prior to another daring stunt. Blondin revealed that having crossed with an empty wheelbarrow, he intended to repeat the trick, only with a man inside it. He asked the reporter, 'Do you believe I can do it?' 'Yes, you can,' the newspaper man replied. 'You are the greatest stunt artist of all time!' 'Right,' challenged Blondin, 'get in the wheelbarrow. Let's go!'

Apparently, the journalist made his excuses and left quickly.

The story shows the difference between belief in a general sense and believing in something so strongly you are willing to risk your life for it.

We are about to enter Holy Week, a special time for Christian believers. It's the time of year when speculative stories tend to circulate in the media along the lines: did the resurrection actually happen?

I read today of one group called 'The Jesus Seminar' in the USA. Organized by ex-clergyman Robert W. Funk, it consists of a group of theologians who meet to discuss if various biblical events occurred. In recent years the virgin birth and the teaching of Jesus have received the collective thumbs down and now, in the seasonal nick of time, they have pronounced the resurrection of Jesus a myth.

In contrast, there are hundreds of fine scholars worldwide who would stake their academic reputations on the fact that Jesus rose again—but that rarely hits the headlines.

Among several pieces of evidence that lead me to the inescapable conclusion that the resurrection did happen, perhaps the most compelling is the disciples' unshakeable conviction that what they saw was not a ghost, an illusion or a wistful memory of a dear friend, but the risen Christ. And many of them were killed for refusing to budge from that belief.

Like Blondin and his wheelbarrow challenge, their actions speak louder than words. Here is a faith in a fact so sure, it was worth dying for.

For further reading

ACTS 27:13–44

Despite Paul's warning, the ship had set sail, only to be overtaken by a ferocious storm. After many days of battering by the storm, everyone had given up hope of surviving but, in the midst of despair, Paul was able to encourage them because God had revealed to him that they would *all* survive. The sailors became fearful that the ship would be broken apart on the rocks, so they decided to save their own lives by escaping in the lifeboat. Paul warned that their attempt to survive would fail unless they took the apparently greater risk of remaining with the ship. 'So the soldiers cut the ropes that held the lifeboat and let it fall away.' They put their faith in what Paul had told them rather than in manmade means of escape. There are times when we try to take precautions or have a fall-back position when God wants us to take a risk for him. We need to 'cut the ropes' of our lifeboats, whatever they are, and move on in faith, knowing that God will meet all our needs.

Prayer

I put my faith in you, risen Lord Jesus. You are my only hope. I trust in you alone because you will not let me down.

Love story

This is love: not that we loved God, but that he loved us and sent his Son as an atoning sacrifice for our sins.

1 JOHN 4:10

Years ago a man walked along Princes Street in Edinburgh and spotted an impressive window display of some paintings. One of the pictures, entitled *Crucifixion*, portrayed the death of Jesus Christ.

The man was transfixed. It was not simply the artist's skill that made him stop, but that the painting stirred within him some long-forgotten memories.

Suddenly he realized that he wasn't alone. A small boy was standing nearby, staring at the same painting. As their eyes met, the boy launched into an uninvited explanation. 'That's Jesus, sir, on the cross. They nailed him there with that crown of thorns on his head and they killed him. He was a good man who died for us. That's his mother standing there, watching what they did to him.' The man felt a lump rise in his throat. The lad continued, 'He died to pay for our sins and then they buried him yonder.'

It was too real for the man, who simply nodded and walked away. He had only gone a few yards when he felt a tug at his coat. Turning, he saw the boy, who blurted out breathlessly, 'I forgot to tell you, sir. I forgot to tell you he rose again!'

Any account of the Easter event that omits the earth-shattering message of the empty tomb of Jesus has no good news to offer. So pivotal is the resurrection of Jesus to his claim to be the Son of God, that Paul, the Christian leader, bluntly declared, 'If Christ has not been raised, our preaching is useless and so is your faith' (1 Corinthians 15:14).

I read a book some years ago, entitled *The Empty Cross of Jesus* (R.T.

France, IVP). I was sure the author had made a mistake and meant to write about the empty tomb instead. I read the book and discovered the point.

We are not invited to follow the example of a dead Messiah, who simply left a legacy of a life of love. Rather, we are called to discover the only one to bankrupt death and strip away its power. As Jesus said, 'I am the First and the Last. I am the Living One; I was dead, and behold I am alive for ever and ever! And I hold the keys of death and Hades' (Revelation 1:17–18).

The little boy got it right. You need the whole story to complete the picture.

For further reading

1 JOHN 4:7–21

We know the story so well of how Jesus lived and died and rose again, but there are still times when it overwhelms us just as it did when we first heard and believed, as in the story above—or when we see it through the eyes of a child, or when a new Christian shares what Jesus now means to him or her, or perhaps when we are alone with God and he speaks to us anew. In this passage in 1 John, we are reminded that our love for God and others is only possible 'because he *first* loved us'. As Paul expressed it in Romans, 'While we were still sinners, Christ died for us' (5:8). God's love and Jesus' death and resurrection were only the beginning of the story for us: 'And he has given us this command: Whoever loves God must also love his brother' (v. 21).

Prayer

Dear loving Father, some people are very hard to love. Help me to reach out to those I find difficult to love as I seek to obey your command, remembering how you first loved me despite my sinfulness.

Religious fireworks

Seek good, not evil, that you may live. Then the Lord God Almighty
will be with you, just as you say he is.
AMOS 5:14

'It's been the cause of more wars than anything else in the history of the
world,' said the man at the end of the bar. 'Religion,' he almost spat the
word, 'is good for nothing except trouble.' Several nodded in silent
agreement.

'Now, you take this Guy Fawkes business,' the saloon bar sage
continued; 'all these kiddies buying fireworks and burning guys on top
of bonfires, all because a man tried to blow up Parliament. And do you
know why?' No one answered, as it seemed a pity to cut him off in mid-
flow. 'Because he was getting them back for all the persecution of
Roman Catholics by King James I. One lot attacks another lot, so they
try to get their own back; one of them is caught, tortured and executed.
And here we are nearly 400 years later, reliving it all by burning dummy
Guy Fawkes on bonfires and letting off bangers to celebrate. It's all done
in the name of religion and it's barbaric.'

He went quiet, having got it off his chest, for the time being at least.
All eyes turned to me, silent and accusing stares saying nothing and
everything at the same time.

'You're absolutely right,' I began, 'and it's not over yet. Look at all
that ethnic cleansing in Bosnia, or the Troubles in Northern Ireland.
Then there's the Arabs and the Jews in the Middle East—it's all down
to religion.' The audience looked stunned as I dribbled the ball back to
my own goal line. 'Religion can be divisive, bigoted, murderous...' The
ball soared back into an empty net. 'And you know what? God is pretty
cheesed off with it too!' They took on the look of a home crowd with a
goal disallowed in extra time.

I continued, 'There's a bit in the Bible where God says, "I hate, I despise your religious feasts; I cannot stand your assemblies… Away with the noise of your songs!" God says religion without right actions towards others is empty. "But let justice roll on like a river, righteousness like a never-failing stream"' (Amos 5:21, 23, 24).

'You see, faith that doesn't make me a nicer person to live with is not going to make the world a happier place to live in, is it?' A few nods around the bar showed assent.

'You can be religious without being righteous,' I concluded, 'and one without the other is as dangerous as a lighted match dropped in a box of fireworks!'

For further reading

Amos 5:6–27

We can't fool God. Whatever our outward religious observances, our offerings and worship, they are worthless if we seek evil, not good. And neither can we fool the world. It's hardly surprising that religion has a bad name when it is used to justify hatred and injustice. Amos warns us that, for some, the day of the Lord and the return of the risen, victorious Christ will be a day of 'darkness, not light—pitch-dark, without a ray of brightness' (v. 20). We are not called to make God in our own image but to become like him ourselves. Religion that serves our own interests and reinforces our prejudices is not true religion at all. In 2 Corinthians 5:20 Paul says that we are 'Christ's ambassadors, as though God were making his appeal through us,' so he tells us, 'Examine yourselves to see whether you are in the faith; test yourselves' (2 Corinthians 13:5).

Prayer

Lord, shine your righteous light on my life. Illuminate the dark corners where I need to change. Forgive me for the times when I am a poor ambassador for you.

Don't forget

Written for Remembrance Sunday 1994.

So I will always remind you of these things, even though you know them and are firmly established in the truth you now have.
2 PETER 1:12

Standing in a delightfully sunny Cornish cove a few days ago, I was faced with one of those impossible-to-answer-simply questions that small children seem to have a special gift in asking.

'What would have happened if we *hadn't* won the war, Dad?' my youngest inquired.

We had been standing together reading the carefully prepared text detailing how American troops had sailed from Cornwall in 1944 as part of the largest invasion fleet in history. We have been reminded of the details daily over the past week or so: 156,000 men, 1,200 fighting ships, 10,000 planes, 4,126 landing craft, 800 transport ships. In many ways statistics mask the staggering story. But my little boy's question put a different perspective on the D-Day ceremonies for me, at least.

What *if?*

Most clergy under the age of fifty will tell you (if they are honest) that Remembrance Day and associated commemorative events are not the easiest services to conduct. After all, if you have no personal knowledge or experience of war, it is easy to end up sounding very hollow.

But remembrance is an important habit to cultivate and the generation that forgets its past sentences itself to a rootless present.

In the pages of the Old Testament we read that God commanded a memorial mound to be built to commemorate Israel passing into the Promised Land. Part of the purpose of such a monument was, 'In the future, when your children ask you, "What do these stones mean?" tell them…' (Joshua 4:6–7).

My son's question that disturbed a tranquil afternoon was in similar vein. To seek to give an answer was a sobering experience. 'What if?' helps to make sense of the dedication, courage and selfless sense of duty we have heard much of in these past few days.

The children of the new Europe must not be allowed to grow up ignorant of the old Europe. And for that reason, among so many others, it is right and good every year to stand still and remember.

For further reading

2 PETER 1:1–21

As the years pass, the number of people who experienced the two World Wars diminishes. Perhaps one day we will be observing a day of remembrance of wars for which there are no longer any eye-witnesses—although, sadly, there have been many wars since to remind us of their horrors. Jesus came to fight and win the war against sin and death, and Peter was an eye-witness of his ministry, of his death and resurrection, but he had had a revelation that he was soon going to die. Until then he wanted to keep on reminding others of the power of Jesus and their need 'to make your calling and election sure' (v. 10), so that they would not forget, even when he was no longer with them. We too are prone to forget, and we need to be reminded of the freedoms we enjoy, both those that have been preserved for us by the winning of earthly wars and the freedom from the power of death and sin, won for us at such great cost by our Saviour.

Prayer

'Where, O death, is your victory?
Where, O death, is your sting?'
Thank you, Jesus.
1 CORINTHIANS 15:55

No wonder

'Glory to God in the highest, and on earth peace to men on whom
his favour rests.'
LUKE 2:14

'We live in a world with a withered sense of wonder.' Not my words but
those of a man who has walked on the moon and viewed the earth from
space—Colonel James Irwin, the Apollo astronaut.

His comment is a pinpoint assessment of a pygmy generation
drowning in information yet starved of knowledge.

Where has the wonder gone? It is a question worth asking this
Christmas Eve.

You will find it in the face of a child exploding with excitement
tomorrow morning, or through the eyes of friends who have not met for
a time. It's usually present when lovers are lost in each other, and the air
is thick with it when a new baby is born. You discover wonder in strange
places. A few months ago I saw it in an Indian whose village had been
given a well. You can meet it with those close to dying and in people
weighed down with disadvantage.

But the greatest source of wonder is the story of the God-Man, Jesus
of Nazareth. The Bible writers are quite restrained in their choice of
words when recording the birth of Jesus. Not so the angels. These
heavenly beings can't keep quiet as they witness the most remarkable
thing they have known. Heaven's curtains part and the skies are filled
with what must have been a virtuoso performance. 'Glory to God in the
highest, and on earth peace to men on whom his favour rests' was the
theme song.

Now *that* is wonder.

Before you dismiss this as the stuff of fairy tales, think again. Wonder
does not mean thinking fluffy thoughts about a make-believe world.

James Irwin, who lamented our withered sense of wonder, was a committed Christian who marvelled not just at the mystery of our universe, but in its Maker. And he is not alone. Albert Einstein acknowledged, 'I only trace the lines that flow from God.'

But let me leave the last word on Christmas Eve to Robert Boyd, former Professor of Astrophysics at University College, London. In a poem entitled 'Creation', specially written for Christmas, he wrote:

> *The mystery of being, still unsolved*
> *By all our science and philosophy,*
> *Fills me with breathless wonder, and the God*
> *From whom it all continually proceeds*
> *Calls forth my worship and shall worship have.*
> *But love in incarnation draws my soul*
> *To humble adoration of a Babe;*
> *'In this was manifest the love of God.'*

For further reading

ISAIAH 9:2–7

A man in the vast reaches of space must feel very small. He must wonder that he is there at all. This passage in Isaiah foretells the wonder of the first Christmas and all that that will mean. The light of God's salvation dawned gradually on us, the people 'living in the land of the shadow of death' (v. 2). We have yet to see the full blaze of its glory when Jesus comes again. Isaiah speaks first of the effect of the coming of the Messiah when there will be great rejoicing and freedom from oppression, an end to war and everlasting peace. And then he says the breathtaking words that have echoed down the centuries: 'For to us a child is born, to us a son is given' and tells us the beautiful names of our Saviour: 'Wonderful Counsellor, Mighty God, Everlasting Father, Prince of Peace' (v. 6). All the wonder of God's love is expressed to us in the long-planned birth of a tiny baby.

> *Praise, my soul, the king of heaven,*
> *To his feet thy tribute bring.*
> J. GOSS (1800–1880)

Windows on the
Ten Commandments

Ten suggestions?

But whoever listens to me will live in safety and be at ease, without fear of harm.

PROVERBS 1:33

I have long thought that Church authorities ought to have similar powers to the sporting bodies who charge errant members with 'bringing the game into disrepute'. I'm not simply talking about the usual 'vicar's wife runs off with choirmistress' type of incident, but those occasions when people who purport to be leaders of the Christian community open their mouths and create confusion and damage as a result.

A few days ago, a national newspaper asked a selection of clergymen if they could recall from memory the Ten Commandments. Only 34 per cent could. Allowing for the fact that the question may have come at a busy time of day when other matters were pressing, you may charitably suppose that not every orthopaedic surgeon could name each bone in the body at the drop of a scalpel. But what worried me (and, I suspect, many others) was a comment from a senior clergyman that 'the Ten Commandments are not terribly important for Christians living today. They do not answer the real moral problems affecting modern society.'

After choking on my cornflakes at that little gem, I began to give it serious thought. Perhaps that is why so many churches have become a less efficient extension of the Social Services with a few hymns and prayers thrown in. A colleague in a neighbouring church, reflecting on the same article, commented, 'Some people would be more comfortable if we called them the Ten Suggestions instead of the Ten Commandments!'

Never one to let a challenge go begging, I have reached a decision. Over the next ten studies I will look at each of the commandments in an attempt to demonstrate how relevant they are to a modern world desperately needing a moral framework. You can judge for yourself if they have passed their sell-by date. It is not an easy task with a 400-word limit, but God managed on less, so we'll give it a go.

I'm reminded of the story of the religious sceptic, Voltaire, who, as he was dying, was visited by a priest. Asking, with some surprise, why the priest had bothered to call, he heard the clergyman reply, 'God sent me'—to which Voltaire responded, 'Ah, my dear sir, and where are your credentials?'

At such times, religious clothes and titles cut little ice. It's an authority greater than our own opinion that's called for.

For further reading

PROVERBS 1:20–33

It's not surprising that a cursory reading of the Ten Commandments, with their repetition of 'You shall not...', leads some people to think that they are negative and restrictive. A closer look, however, shows that they are in fact quite the opposite. They are about having healthy family relationships and right priorities. They teach us to be content with what we have and show us how to live balanced lives, with adequate rest from work and time for worship. Above all, they're about putting God first and having an eternal perspective on things. Wouldn't it be wonderful to live in a society with those kind of priorities? The passage in the book of Proverbs is a timely warning to those who choose to ignore God's wise instructions for living, that 'they will eat the fruit of their ways' (v. 31). Far from restricting us, observing the Ten Commandments enables us to live life to the full as God intended.

Prayer

Thank you, Creator God, for giving us the freedom to choose to live lives that please you, build up other people and bring us satisfaction and joy. Help us to see how positive your Commandments are and to keep them and to encourage others to do the same.

Other gods

I am the Lord your God, who brought you out of Egypt, out of the land of slavery. You shall have no other gods before me.

EXODUS 20:2–3

Occasionally I am involved in something out of the ordinary.

Something took place a few days ago that will live with me for a long time. I had the privilege of leading a group of two hundred couples through a renewal of their marriage vows—in the middle of a car park!

This unique event took place in Minehead towards the end of a week-long conference attended by 9,000 Christians of all denominations. The suggestion was made that couples might like to renew their wedding vows, but so many took up the idea that there was no room to accommodate them. Hasty arrangements were made to hold an open-air service in the car park and I found myself perched on a wobbly table, leading them through a brief but moving renewal of vows.

A letter in today's post from one south-west couple says, 'We were delighted to be able to renew our marriage vows. It is our silver wedding anniversary year and we have many changes in our lives to cope with… we are at a real turning point in our married life. The starlit night and Halle Bop in full view was the perfect setting—a moment to cherish…'

So what has all this to do with the first of the Ten Commandments that we reach today? It reads, 'I am the Lord your God, who brought you out of Egypt, out of the land of slavery. You shall have no other gods before me.'

Is this the selfish demand of a petty-minded tribal god? The opening sentence reveals that this is far from the case. God acted in Israel's history by delivering them from a life of slavery in a foreign country. Three and a half thousand years later, that great exodus is still commemorated by the Jewish nation.

The first Commandment sets the tone for all the other nine. It is written in the language of love. When God demands our exclusive attention, it is because he has the right to. He made us, died to bring us into a new relationship and always stands ready to help.

Those couples in the car park, celebrating marriage and renewing their promises to each other, helped me understand why God should insist on our single-minded attention.

It's called the loyalty of love.

For further reading

JEREMIAH 31:3; PSALM 139:1–24

You may have come to a personal faith in God quite recently or you may have walked with him for many years, but however long God has been a part of your life, through Jeremiah God tells us that he has loved us 'with an everlasting love'. Psalm 139 tells us that God was intimately concerned with us even while we were still in the womb, long before we were able to acknowledge him. Even then God had a plan for our lives. He is not capricious and demanding; his love for us is firm and unchanging. He is interested in every detail of our lives; he is 'familiar with all my ways' (Psalm 139:3). The First Commandment asks only what it is natural that we should do: give first place in our lives to the One who loves us more than anyone else ever could and who was willing to pay the price of that love by dying on the cross to save us, undeserving as we are.

Prayer

When I consider your great love for me, Lord, even from the moment of my conception, I am overwhelmed. There are no words to express how much I owe to you. You deserve first place in my life. Forgive me for the times when I forget or choose not to remember this.

Worshipping idols

You shall not make for yourself an idol in the form of anything in heaven above or on the earth beneath or in the waters below. You shall not bow down to them or worship them; for I, the Lord your God, am a jealous God.

EXODUS 20:4

If you have been following our look at the Ten Commandments and their relevance today, you may have thought that number two in the list is a fairly safe bet to be classified as 'no longer important'. It reads, 'You shall not make for yourself an idol...'

The ancient nation of Israel was surrounded by countries that embraced idol-worship as part of everyday life. With a multi-faith hypermarket on offer, it made sense that Israel's God demanded total loyalty from his followers.

But, in today's hi-tech Western world, few bow down to totem poles or have a pet god commemorated by a shrine in the kitchen. Surely here is one commandment that fails the relevance test.

But two important points must not be forgotten. First, Israel's God is not confined to one national grouping. He is God of all and his demand for loyalty applies to all. Second, idolatry is alive and well in Britain today. As writer Joy Davidman pointed out, 'What shape is an idol? Need it be man shape or a beast shape? May it not be any possible shape man can devise—anything from a dynamo to a mink coat—as long as you look to it for your salvation?'

An idol is anything that takes the place of God in our affections. Every Sunday morning, services of worship take place in driveways as the family 'god' is rinsed and waxed. Some have a shrine in the corner of the living-room with our one-eyed 'god' blaring out a daily diet of entertainment and information. Then there's the god Jesus nicknamed

'Mammon', referring to money and possessions that we trust more than God. Even churches aren't immune to idol-worship. Traditions, buildings and systems have a nasty habit of becoming an end in themselves and, instead of pointing us to God, they can end up leading us away from him.

The Old Testament prophets were scathing in pointing out the foolishness of offering devotion to a lump of wood or stone. They are useless. Jeremiah says idols are 'like a scarecrow in a melon patch' (Jeremiah 10:5).

As a fish was made to live in the environment of water, as the car was built to run on petrol, so human beings were designed to live in friendship with the God who created us. Anything else is a poor replacement.

And as the advert says, 'Accept no substitutes.'

For further reading

Isaiah 44:9–23

The logic of this passage in Isaiah is unanswerable. How can something made of a material so ordinary that we use it as firewood without a second thought be endued with god-like qualities? Yet it is not so unusual these days to fall into superstitious ways of thinking. What about the sportsman who always wears the same pair of 'lucky' socks for an important tournament? Or the woman who is made uncomfortable all day because she has forgotten to put on the piece of jewellery she always wears? We are perilously close to having idols when we endow an object with special qualities just because of who gave it to us or what happened to us when it was in our possession. Whenever our minds are distracted from God and our dependence on him, let us be reminded of God's word through Isaiah: 'I have swept away your offences like a cloud, your sins like the morning mist. Return to me, for I have redeemed you' (v. 22).

Prayer

Show me, dear Lord, if I have allowed anything to come before you in my life. Thank you for the assurance of your word that when I turn back to you, you will forgive me.

God's name is special

You shall not misuse the name of the Lord your God, for the Lord will not hold anyone guiltless who misuses his name.

EXODUS 20:7

A young boy returned home from school and reported that a visitor to morning assembly had sworn not once, but repeatedly, and none of the staff seemed to notice or care. An anxious mother contacted the headteacher for an explanation.

It transpired that the visitor to the school assembly was a local minister and, after gentle questioning, the boy reported that the man had continually said, 'Jesus Christ'. Sadly, the only context in which he'd heard the name was as a swear word and he had no concept that it was the name of a real person.

The third of the Ten Commandments says, 'You shall not misuse the name of the Lord your God, for the Lord will not hold anyone guiltless who misuses his name.'

Misusing God's name covers more than expletives. Insincere taking of an oath, false prophecy and using God's name to justify a course of action could all be seen as breaking the third Commandment.

But why the fuss? After all, a word is just a word, isn't it? And using the name of Jesus as a swear word is little more than a verbal punctuation mark, surely?

In the culture of the Bible, a person's name was more than an identification label. It conveyed their whole character—and to abuse or misuse their name was to demean the individual.

In today's society, little is sacred or special. I grew up as a child of the sixties when cynicism took on a fashionable meaning. The Church, politics and the Royal Family were all seen as 'game for a laugh'—and probably the pricking of some pompous bubbles was a healthy thing.

But with that incoming tide, all sorts of destructive driftwood piled on to the beach, not least the pervasive use of blasphemy.

We have laws that govern sexual and racial discrimination—quite rightly. But what about the protection of God's name? 'He's big enough to look after himself,' the critic replies. Quite so. But try using the name of Buddha as a frequent swear word in a play, or make discriminatory remarks about black people in a TV soap, and watch the fallout.

Blasphemy matters, not simply because it offends tens of thousands of citizens of our country who happen to prize religious faith as something special. Far more than that, it offends the God who made us and gave the gift of life.

For further reading

ACTS 4:1–20

The religious leaders in Jerusalem must have been very disturbed when they saw the following that Jesus now had, especially considering their involvement in his death. It was obvious that 'unschooled, ordinary men' could not perform miracles, or show courage when faced with opposition and questioning as Peter and John did, unless there was some special explanation. The rulers, elders and teachers of the law put aside their personal differences and called a special meeting to discuss their problem. They realized that they couldn't stop what was happening unless they could get the apostles to give up speaking and teaching in the name of Jesus. When they forbade them to continue as they were doing, Peter and John refused, choosing to obey God rather than human beings. The name of Jesus, then and now, is unique: 'There is no other name under heaven given to men by which we must be saved' (v. 12). We need to realize afresh the power there is in the name of Jesus.

Prayer

Help me, Almighty God, to treat your name with reverence, and show me how to live in the power of your name so that others will be drawn to want to know you for themselves.

God's special day

Remember the Sabbath day by keeping it holy.
EXODUS 20:8

Anna Sewell's classic novel, *Black Beauty*, has entranced readers since its publication in 1877. The hero of the story, Black Beauty, spent his declining years working as cabman Jerry Barker's horse in London. At one point, Jerry talks about problems faced by cabmen who couldn't afford to take Sundays off. Barker shows himself a man of principle in defending Sunday as a day of rest, and says, 'If a thing is right, it can be done, and if it is wrong, it can be done without...'

The fourth of the Ten Commandments says, 'Remember the Sabbath day by keeping it holy.' God's laws make sense in building a better world but what's the point of making one day in seven special?

The principle goes back to creation, when God rested on the seventh day. He didn't need to rest because he was tired, but he modelled the principle of rest as a pattern for his creation to imitate. The 'rest day' was for our good.

Just as in the 24-hour cycle we need a period of sleep, so within the demands of a week a specific period of time is needed for rest. You don't need a Bible to tell you that. Listen to a distinguished physician, Sir James Chrichton-Browne: 'We doctors in the treatment of nervous diseases are now constantly compelled to prescribe periods of rest. Some periods are, I think, only Sundays in arrears.'

Tragically 'Sabbath observance' has been haunted by the same type of legalistic killjoys that clashed with Jesus. He answered his critics, 'The Sabbath was made for man, not man for the Sabbath' (Mark 2:27).

This was no prison to restrict us but an open place designed to enrich us.

God's idea in giving a special day in the week can be summed up in three words: rest (from the daily routine of work), renewal (as we find God through worship) and recreation (as we deepen ties with family and friends).

Our helter-skelter lifestyles tell us that this is great in principle but impossible in practice. Really? Jerry Barker was right when he said, 'If a thing is right, it can be done...'

And on Easter Sunday, we recall that Jesus broke the death barrier on the first day of the week and, ever since, Christians have called it 'the Lord's Day'.

What better day to worship God—and find ourselves again.

For further reading

MATTHEW 6:25–34

When we are conscientious about making one day a week special and taking time to worship God, to spend time with the most important people in our lives and to rest from our usual activities, we are making a healthy choice, right now and in eternal terms. Jesus' recipe for living a worry-free life is to have the right priorities: 'Seek first his kingdom and his righteousness...' (v. 33). He does not want us to spend time fretting over our physical need for food and clothes as those who do not know God as heavenly Father do. We can be assured that God will provide all we need if we make it our first aim to serve and please him. It is easy to get caught up in the way the world thinks when we go about our hectic, everyday lives. We can use Sundays (or, if we are obliged to work on a Sunday, our day off) as an opportunity to readjust priorities that have gone askew during a busy week. God wants to use the Sabbath to bless us, if we are willing to let him.

Prayer

Help me, Father, to discover the rest, recreation and renewal that you want me to enjoy when I order my life according to your wise instructions.

Honour your parents

Written at the start of the General Election campaign in 1997.

Honour your father and your mother, so that you may live long in the land the Lord your God is giving you.

EXODUS 20:12

The General Election campaign is under way. Among various claims, counter-claims and promises made over the next six weeks, I hope that one issue will get more than a passing mention: the family.

How does the family landscape in Britain look today?

- Less than two in five households are made up of a husband, wife and children.
- Almost as many again are headed by a lone parent or single person.
- By 2000, one in three of the UK population will be in one-parent households.
- Over 1000 children a week lose contact with their fathers.
- 400 children per day see their parents divorce.

Yet the United Nations Universal Declaration of Human Rights states, 'The family is the natural and fundamental group unit of society.' Politicians who claim concern for our communities would do well to seek ways of strengthening families. Respect for authority, developing a sense of responsibility and learning to love and be loved are basic concepts that we begin to learn not at school but at home. Matthew Taylor Coleridge wrote, 'In today already walks tomorrow.'

Number five in the list of the Ten Commandments reads: 'Honour your father and mother, so that you may live long in the land the Lord your God is giving you.' The Hebrew word 'honour' means to give esteem and the Jewish Talmud makes the strong assertion, 'We are to revere our parents as God.'

That comes across as tough if your parents have mistreated you and it is certainly not to be used as a cloak to cover up sexual, emotional or physical abuse in the home. God's principle is that parents are to be honoured because the family unit is the basic building block of society.

But parents must be worthy of honour by creating high-quality relationships that provide a model for children to copy. What children see, they become, and it is easier to respect parents who respect each other.

Personal faith, as opposed to a vague nominal religious belief, has its part to play. A teenager who committed suicide in New York left a note, part of which read, 'My parents brought me up to believe in God, and to believe that he doesn't matter.'

The Ten Commandments are not an outmoded list of rules from the past, but a living reminder of a God who cares—and matters.

For further reading

COLOSSIANS 3:12—4:6

As Paul implies in this passage by his admonition to fathers not to 'embitter' their children, every parent is imperfect. Some, of course, are much more so than others. But the Fifth Commandment is addressed to *all* who have parents, without exception. In the passage in Colossians, Paul gives a hint of how to honour parents who are not worthy of our respect. He says, 'Children, obey your parents in everything, *for this pleases the Lord*' (v. 20). We do not honour them (or obey them) for their sake but for our heavenly Father's sake. Other sections of this passage have great relevance to the way in which we are to honour them: we are to treat them with 'compassion, kindness, humility, gentleness and patience' (v. 12) and to 'forgive whatever grievances' we have against them (v. 13). And God, our loving Father who never lets us down, will see and be pleased with us.

Prayer

If your parents hurt or abused you in any way, thank God that he understands and loves you in a way no earthly parent ever could.

If you have been blessed with parents who love you and have won your respect, thank God and ask him to show you some way in which you can express to them your appreciation.

No killing

Written on the first anniversary of the Dunblane School murders.

You shall not murder (Exodus 20:13)

Tragedy has a habit of leaving a one-word legacy. Mention Aberfan or Hillsborough and sad memories come flooding back. A year ago another name was added to the national psyche—Dunblane.

This week we have thought of that small community as they share in grief and remembrance. For us, life goes on; for them, it will never be the same again.

My attempt to prove the relevance of the Ten Commandments has now reached number six in the list: 'You shall not murder.' In Hebrew only two terse words are used: 'No killing.'

Behind this commandment lies an important God-given principle: life is sacred and must be treated with special care. Most would agree that this makes sense, and any humane society frames its laws to protect the right to life. But is the obvious really obvious?

In the current debate on abortion, those who take a pro-life view point to the 'sanctity of life' principle as their driving force. They take the Sixth Commandment as the foundation for their case. Cardinal Thomas Winning in Scotland made a bold offer last weekend to provide financial help to women contemplating abortion. This was no cheap publicity stunt but a serious offer born out of a desire to offer a practical alternative to women forced into a heart-rending decision through financial need. He said, 'Goodness has not been extinguished. We can still fashion a civilization of love, a society where "care" does not mean "kill".'

The application of the principle extends to other areas of life. The subject of euthanasia will increasingly feature in public debate in the next few years; the link between violence portrayed in the media and its influence on behaviour continues to be discussed; gun laws and the availability of other weapons is an issue that will not go away quietly.

It seems that the commandment 'No killing' is not confined to dusty archives, nor should it be for any society that dares to call itself civilized.

The right to life is the most fundamental of all human rights. And surely there could be no better tribute to the slaughtered innocents of Dunblane than to ensure that at every level of British society we examine ourselves to see how seriously we take the precious gift of life—and do all in our power to protect it.

For further reading

MATTHEW 5:21–24; JAMES 4:1–3

In the Sermon on the Mount, Jesus expounded the commandment against murder, explaining that it includes the heart attitude that can lead to murder but may be expressed by anger against another. James talks about this in his letter when he is addressing relationships within the church: 'You kill and covet... You quarrel and fight' (James 4:2). Murder may be 'the last thing on our minds' but in allowing ourselves to hate or to be angry without resolving the matter, we are opening the door to even worse things. Whenever we abuse our power over another person or act hatefully toward them, whether it be an unborn child, the elderly and sick, a member of our family or just someone we disagree with, we are going against the spirit of the Sixth Commandment. Jesus says that we need to make it a matter of urgency to deal with any problem that has come between us and someone else.

Prayer

Lord, I would be horrified if anyone suggested I were capable of murder but Jesus' words leave me without a leg to stand on. Forgive me for those times when my actions towards others are motivated not by love but by anger, and help me to change.

Holy matrimony

You shall not commit adultery.

EXODUS 20:14

A group of builders demolishing a church building were under orders to preserve anything valuable. A workman came across a stone slab on which the Ten Commandments had been engraved. He asked his foreman's advice. 'Chuck it out!' he was told. 'They don't bother with them any more.'

Today we reach the seventh of the Ten Commandments, which reads, 'You shall not commit adultery.'

You don't have to be religious to have concern about the breakdown of marriage in modern Britain. *Population Trends* (produced by a Government agency) makes disturbing reading:

- The divorce rate is now approaching one in two marriages.
- Less than 50 per cent of married couples will celebrate their silver wedding anniversary.
- Government spends £4–6 million per day on the costs of broken marriages.
- The NHS spends £100 million per annum on illness linked to marriage breakdown.

Leave economic arguments and consider the human costs. Hardly a week of my life passes without being confronted by the personal pain of divorce. Broken marriages produce broken people.

Divorce is often caused by a variety of complex reasons and a proper Christian response is compassion rather than judgment. But if you are involved in picking up people who have fallen over the edge of a cliff, isn't it reasonable to ask why no one has thought of putting a fence at the top?

The Commandments are not intended to curb freedom but to give a framework in which freedom can be enjoyed. Keeping a marriage vow is an important aspect of what is often missing today—commitment—the moral cement which holds life together.

This week, Rabbi Jonathan Sacks has published *The Politics of Hope* (Cape, 1997). He makes this thought-provoking comment about adultery: 'If marriage is holy, adultery is a sin. If it is moral, then adultery is wrong. Adultery is wrong because it is a betrayal—of a partner, a commitment, a promise, a trust.'

Concern for physical health has climbed to the top of our national agenda. Information on heart disease, the dangers of smoking, excessive drinking and the need for exercise is freely promoted and taught in schools. Most would agree that this is a good thing.

But our emotional and spiritual well-being is equally important and perhaps the need is greater than ever for an honest re-examination of the Maker's instructions.

For further reading

2 SAMUEL 11:1–17

Instead of going out to war with his men, David had sent his army off under Joab's command and stayed behind in Jerusalem. Perhaps he was spending his time just lazing around, with all the men away and no company to relieve his boredom. At any rate, we are told that he got up from his bed 'one evening' and saw a beautiful woman bathing. Bathsheba was a distraction he thought he could get away with. Even after she became pregnant, he believed he could cover up what they had done. But he had not reckoned on Uriah's sense of what was right. This, in the end, led to Uriah's barely disguised murder in battle and the death of the baby. It's a sorry story with nothing to redeem it and the consequences were played out through the remainder of David's life. The act of adultery might look enticing at the time but one thing will always lead to another. We should beware lest the consequences of short-lived pleasure are something we have to live with regretfully for the rest of our lives.

Prayer

Bring before God the names of anyone known to you—husbands, wives, children—who are suffering the pain of broken marriages or troubled relationships.

If you yourself have been responsible for a broken marriage, thank God that he has not stopped loving you. Ask him to bring healing to those you have hurt.

Don't steal

Written in March 1997, following the conclusion of the largest corruption trial involving an Inland Revenue official.

You shall not steal.
EXODUS 20:15

The *Wall Street Journal* reported how someone has estimated that 35 million laws have been placed on the statute books trying to enforce the Ten Commandments. If nothing else, it underlines their importance as foundation stones for civilized life as we know it.

Today we reach Commandment number eight: 'You shall not steal.' If you remember, this all began when I objected to the ludicrous assertion that the Commandments have no relevance to modern society.

This week has seen news of the biggest corruption scandal ever faced by the Inland Revenue. Michael Allcock, a senior taxman, has been jailed and other staff face disciplinary action. Months of proceedings and mountains of paper can be summarized in a phrase: *don't steal*.

Figures show that each month over 50,000 people in the UK are burgled and that £120 is added to our annual shopping bill to cover the cost of theft. Our burglary rate is one of the highest in Europe and theft from shops, post offices and petrol stations totals over £2 billion annually. *Don't steal*.

In a survey, Gallup discovered that eight out of ten Britons live in fear of burglary and almost half the population has installed extra security in recent years. Crime costs each person in Britain the equivalent of £10 per week and police estimate that a third of all thefts are committed to pay for drugs. *Don't steal*.

Most of us have a sad theft story to tell. Here's mine. A young couple, struggling to get by each month, bought some secondhand baby equipment. Doing a favour for a severely disabled friend, they popped around to his home. In a matter of minutes, as they played Good Samaritans, their car was broken into and all the baby equipment was stolen. That was in Plymouth a few weeks before Christmas. *Don't steal.*

And just in case we feel smug in our outrage, how quick are we to point out that we've been given too much change, or to be accurate in our tax returns or forgetful in returning things that are borrowed? *Don't steal.*

For further reading

EPHESIANS 4:17—5:2

The book of Ephesians overflows with good advice about living the Christian life. We have not been saved so that we might carry on sinning with impunity but so that we can live lives that please God. We are to have a new attitude, in fact a whole 'new self, created to be like God in true righteousness and holiness' (4:24). In these verses Paul says that 'he who has been stealing must steal no longer' (4:28) but, in case we think that lets us out, he doesn't stop there. The former thief is to find work so that he can fill his time productively. And that work is not to provide solely for his own needs but so that 'he may have something to share with those in need' (4:28). The selfishness of stealing is to be replaced with a positive attitude of generosity toward others. Even if we believe ourselves to be keeping the Commandment by not stealing, it is worth examining how far we are characterized by generosity.

Prayer

Heavenly Father, Paul's words give me no reason to be complacent just because I do not steal. Open my eyes to the needs of others and help me to live open-handedly towards them.

Tell the truth

You shall not give false testimony against your neighbour.

EXODUS 20:16

As someone who often writes job references, I was interested to read an article explaining how to write a good reference for a bad employee without lying. Here's a taster:

'You will be fortunate to get this person to work for you' = *Best of luck, I never succeeded in getting anything out of him.*

'A woman who is hard to find' = *She is never at her desk when you need her.*

'One of the most discriminating people you'll ever meet' = *Fussy and bigoted.*

'A seasoned employee' = *Frequently pickled after lunch.*

Apart from raising a smile, it also raised a question: when is not telling the whole truth equal to not telling the truth at all? Number nine of the Ten Commandments reads, 'You shall not give false testimony against your neighbour.'

It conjures up images of a law court and the seriousness of lying under oath. We value this so highly that it is enshrined in our law as the criminal offence of perjury. But does the Commandment only apply to telling the truth in a courtroom? Reading through the rest of the Bible, it appears that the Maker's instructions cover integrity in our words in every area of life. They challenge gossip and malicious half-truths as well as deliberate lies and they apply equally in the living-room or saloon bar as they do in a law court.

If you have been the victim of a misunderstanding, particularly if false information has been given, you will know how destructive it can be. A lie spoken in a minute can take a lifetime to live down.

Do God's laws make sense? Think of the alternatives. Lying in a court of law can lead to an injustice. Lying in a relationship can lead to a breakdown of trust. Lying at work can lead to a loss of reputation. And lying in a matter of public interest can lead to a loss of confidence.

By contrast, imagine a world that is just, where a person's word can be relied upon absolutely—a world that doesn't feed on the dark poison of lies, where truth is not laughed at but honoured. As Winston Churchill expressed it, 'Truth is incontrovertible. Panic may resent it; ignorance may deride it; malice may distort it; but there it is.' Oh, for a world where truth gets a chance.

Heaven on earth? Precisely.

For further reading

Psalm 109:1–31

Very few of us will ever find ourselves in a position where we will be tempted to bear false witness against our neighbour in court. However, all of us face the temptation to be less than fair and honest about other people almost daily. In conversation we may tend to exaggerate the good things about ourselves, even if that makes others look worse than they are, particularly when we feel we have been mistreated. In this psalm, David describes how it feels to be on the receiving end of this kind of unfairness. It's worth trying to put ourselves in the other person's shoes before we say anything negative about them. There are almost always two (or more) sides to any story and we should be guarded in the way we speak and the things we say. We should remember, as the Bible says in Ecclesiastes 3:7, that there is 'a time to be silent' as well as 'a time to speak'.

Prayer

Teach me, Lord, always to speak honestly and fairly of others and to know the times when it is better to say nothing at all. Thank you that you will one day vindicate me for the things that have been wrongly said of me.

Be content

You shall not covet your neighbour's house. You shall not covet
your neighbour's wife, or his manservant or maidservant, his ox or
donkey, or anything that belongs to your neighbour.

EXODUS 20:17

In August 1963, Ronnie Biggs took part in what became known as the
Great Train Robbery. £2.5 million was stolen in the raid and Biggs was
quickly caught and jailed for thirty years. After only fifteen months of his
sentence, he escaped and since 1970 has lived as a fugitive from justice
in Brazil. A few years ago, Biggs was interviewed by a national newspaper. One of the questions put to him was, 'When and where were
you happiest?' Biggs' reply makes sobering reading: 'Living in Redhill,
Surrey, with my wife and children in early 1963.'

One of life's emptiest experiences comes when, after giving everything to get what you want most, you find that what you wanted is not
what you needed.

Number ten in the list of the Ten Commandments reads, 'You shall
not covet your neighbour's house. You shall not covet your neighbour's
wife, or his manservant or maidservant, his ox or donkey, or anything
that belongs to your neighbour.' In case we feel comforted that oxen and
donkeys are not exactly high on our 'most needed' list at the moment,
it's worth remembering that to covet means to be controlled by a deep,
burning desire to have what belongs to someone else. And that covers a
Skoda as well as a servant.

Wrapping it up in plain English, it means greed—greed for money,
position, possessions, even people. So what's the harm in wanting?
Simply that it warps the value of things, spoils relationships, causes
arguments, breeds selfishness and, left unchecked, can lead to violent
crime. Most of all, it's like a mirage in a desert. We don't end up happier,

just hungrier. As the German philosopher Schopenhauer described coveting: 'It is like sea water: the more we drink, the thirstier we become.'

It may not make the ad-men richer, but we would all be less uptight if we learned to take the wanting out of wanting. Poet Steve Turner sums it up neatly:

Poor

I thought I was poor.
I mean,
nowhere left to stack the videos.
Then I realized
there are people
in the world
who don't even have shelves.

For further reading

GENESIS 27:30–41

Jacob wasn't an attractive character. His covetousness led him into deceiving his father and stealing what, by rights, belonged to his brother. The consequences were that Esau became murderously angry, and Jacob had to leave his home and family and flee for his life. This attitude of wanting what belonged to someone else did not end there but spilled over into the next generation as well. Jacob's own sons mirrored his covetous behaviour and plotted to murder their brother Joseph because they envied his position as favourite and indulged son. Jacob's whole life and the relationships within his family were marred by the effects of covetousness acted upon. We should be very careful that our desire to have what belongs to someone else does not take over our lives, spoiling our relationships and blinding us to the blessings that God has given specifically to us.

Prayer

Father, teach us to be content with what we have. Help us not to be so obsessed with what other people have that we miss the many blessings you have lavished upon us.

Windows on Life

Creation in reverse

God saw all that he had made, and it was very good. And there was evening, and there was morning—the sixth day. Thus the heavens and the earth were completed in all their vast array.

GENESIS 1:31—2:1

Every now and then, you come across something that really makes you stop and think. A few days ago, I read this piece written by a university student. It is entitled 'Creation in Reverse':

Man said, "Let there be power.' And there was power; and man saw that the power looked good. He called those who sought power 'great leaders'. The evening and morning were the sixth day.

Then man said, 'Let there be a division among all peoples and divide those who are for my power from those who are against my power.' And it was so. The hostile people he called 'them' and the friendly people he called 'us'. The evening and morning were the fifth day.

Then man said, 'Let us gather our power together in one place and create one empire of control—brain-washing and indoctrination to control men's minds, militia and secret police to control men's behaviour, myths and symbols to control men's emotions.' And it was so. The evening and morning were the fourth day.

Then man said, 'Let there be censorship to divide the propaganda from the truth.' And he made two great bureaux, one to write the news for those at home and the other to write the news for those abroad. And it was so. The evening and morning were the third day.

Then man said, 'Let us make weapons of destruction which can destroy every form of life that moves on the face of the earth and in the sea.' So man made weapons of war, missiles and bombs, lethal germs and chemicals. He called this arsenal 'defences and deterrents'. The evening and morning were the second day.

Then man said, 'Let us make God in our own image and let him take the blame for the suffering we shall cause.' So man made God in his own image, in the image of man created he them. And he said, 'Rampage unfettered and extend your dominion over the whole earth. Shatter the peace, rape the environment, exploit, oppress and kill.' So man saw all that he had made and behold it was very, very bad. There was evening and morning, the last day.

As I said, every now and then you read something that really makes you stop and think… and then pray.

For further reading

ROMANS 8:18–27; REVELATION 21:1–5

Environmental disasters are often reported on the news; war is never out of it—only the locations vary; famine and disease are commonplace. We live in a world that seems out of control, where wickedness seems to flourish. And yet the Bible reminds us that 'the creation itself will be liberated from its bondage to decay' (Romans 8:21). We are able to look forward to a time when 'there will be no more death or mourning or crying or pain, for the old order of things has passed away' (Revelation 21:4). We have God's promise: 'I am making everything new! … These words are trustworthy and true' (Revelation 21:5). Human beings got it wrong in the first place but God will put it gloriously right in the end. In the meantime, God's Holy Spirit will show us how we should pray.

Prayer

Thank you, Creator God, for the beauty of all that you have made and for the ability you have given us to enjoy your creation. Help us to be responsible in the way we use the resources you have given to us.

Which destination?

There is a way that seems right to a man, but in the end it leads to death.

PROVERBS 14:12

Remember those jokes about good old British Rail and long delays caused by leaves on the track? Well, remember them with affection and be thankful that at least you usually arrived where you wanted to go, even if later than planned.

If you travelled on Northwest Airlines Flight 52 on 5 September 1995, you would not have been so lucky. The DC10 was due to fly from Detroit to Frankfurt only it... er... didn't. Instead it landed 200 miles away in Brussels, which was the right continent but the wrong country.

It wasn't bad weather or overcrowded airways that led to the change of destination. It was such a serious error that the crew were suspended while the US Federal Aviation Administration launched a detailed investigation.

Somewhere along the line, the plane was assigned the wrong destination, either on the flight deck or through an error by air traffic control. To make matters worse, passengers knew they were heading for the wrong destination via an electronic map in the cabin that plotted the plane's progress. They simply assumed that there was a good reason for landing in Belgium instead of Germany. As one official neatly surmised, 'The only people on the plane who didn't know where they were, were the three guys up front!'

There is something distinctly unnerving when you end up where you hadn't planned to go—like a businessman I heard of recently who made the weary comment, 'For thirty years I've been climbing a ladder, only to discover that it's propped against the wrong wall.'

The book of Proverbs has many wise and helpful insights. Some of its sharp statements blend with others in pouring refreshingly cool wisdom into scorched, parched lives. 'There is a way that seems right to a man, but in the end it leads to death' is a sobering challenge to avoid an unhealthy 'I did it my way' attitude.

Beyond the warning comes a more positive note: 'Trust in the Lord with all your heart and lean not on your own understanding; in all your ways acknowledge him, and he will make your paths straight' (Proverbs 3:5–6).

Wise advice for everyone's flight deck.

For further reading

ACTS 9:1–25

Saul's experience on the way to Damascus changed his whole life. When he began the journey he was 'breathing out murderous threats against the Lord's disciples' but, after meeting Jesus and preaching so powerfully about him, it was Saul's life that was under threat and he had to make a night-time escape in a basket through a hole in the city wall. From then on, Saul (or Paul) allowed God to choose his destinations, and who could have predicted how greatly God would use him or the places he would visit and the people he would meet? Sometimes we have no choice about where we find ourselves; at other times we need to ask God to show us which choice to make. But whatever our situation may be, we need to rely on God and not on our own limited understanding if we are to live the full and satisfying lives he has planned for us.

Prayer

Wherever I am, Lord, help me to remember that I am your 'chosen instrument' to show Jesus to the people around me. Guard and guide my words and behaviour so that others might want to know him.

Angels unaware!

For we are God's workmanship, created in Christ Jesus to do good works, which God prepared in advance for us to do.
EPHESIANS 2:10

For all their charm, it's no joke when your car breaks down on one of Devon's picturesque country lanes. And it's certainly no joke when night is falling and you can't see where you are.

Travelling home the other evening after a special anniversary dinner, my wife and I found an urgent need to call the RAC. The only problem was, we didn't have a clue where the nearest phone box might be. Leaving the car, we made our way up the dark lane frantically searching for some means of help. We came across a small row of houses, one or two of which still had their lights on. We selected one, knocked on the front door and waited.

Fortunately for us, the door was opened by a couple of angels. Well, not exactly angels—at least, not ones with wings on—but a couple of very understanding people who let us use their phone and tramp mud on their lovely carpet, made us a pot of tea... and then stood with us in the road for fifty minutes until the RAC bowled up. We discussed everything from Desmond Morris and his monkey theories (I'm still puzzling as to why meeting us for the first time prompted that line of discussion) through to the changes in rural Devon since the 'new' A38 was built over two decades ago.

In short, it was a heart-warming experience of real neighbourliness. Getting stuck at that time of night can bring out the worst in you. Finding help in such an unexpected fashion can bring out the best. Maybe that's why the story of the guy who was mugged on the road to Jericho came alive with greater relevance for me last week.

It's not just helping friends that counts, it's helping people you don't know. Admittedly it's a risky business. But, as Jesus pointed out more than once, that's the nature of love.

So, thank you, Kevin and Mary of Bittaford, for being a genuine pair of Good Samaritans. (And sorry about the mud on the carpet!)

For further reading

LUKE 10:25–37

The Good Samaritan happened to be passing at the time. He ignored the danger and inconvenience and took time out from his own plans to help someone in need. Are we prepared to build time into or take time out of our own plans to do the unexpected good works God has prepared in advance for us to do? Or are we so busy reaching our own goals that we have no time to hear God's prompting to do the 'less important' things, like making a phone call or giving time to a stranger who starts a conversation? We cannot *do* anything to inherit eternal life—that is God's free gift to us because of Jesus' sacrificial death on the cross—but we can express our gratitude to God by making our time and our lives more available to him.

Prayer

Ask God to show you those around you who could benefit from some small act of kindness. Ask him to prepare you to meet the unexpected in the day with a willingness to act upon his prompting.

Our Father

I have set the Lord always before me. Because he is at my right hand, I shall not be shaken.

PSALM 16:8

In these days of political correctness everything is under scrutiny—even the Lord's Prayer, as I discovered the other day. Here (if you can bear it) is the politically correct version:

Our Universal Chairperson in Outer Space,

Your identity enjoys the highest rating on a prioritized selectivity scale. May your sphere of influence take on reality parameters, may your mindset be implemented on this planet as in outer space. Allot to us at this point in time, and on a per diem basis, a sufficient and balanced dietary food intake, and rationalize a disclaimer against the negative feedback of others. And deprogramme our negative potentialities, but desensitize the impact of the counter-productive force. For yours is the dominant sphere of influence, the ultimate capability and the highest qualitative rating, at this point in time, and extending beyond a limited time-frame. End of message.

Speaking personally, I much prefer the original. Although popularly called 'the Lord's Prayer', it has been said that a more accurate title would be 'the Disciples' Prayer'. Those friends who were closest to Jesus noticed that he prayed a great deal, often late at night or early in the morning. They probably made the connection that the sense of God's power at work through Jesus was linked to his habit of prayer, so they asked him to teach them how to pray. His response was to give to them (and to us) a remarkably simple and profound prayer (Luke 11:2–4).

It is not a magic formula but rather a model of how to pray. For many it is the first and only prayer they know by heart. And that is exactly where it needs to be prayed from—the heart.

I often meet people who say they don't know how to pray. They feel the need to do it but don't know where to start. Forget the mumbo-jumbo of political correctness and make a start with the prayer Jesus left us.

God has never been fussed about the words we use; it is the attitude of heart that lies behind them that matters most. After all, as someone once said, 'A prayer in its simplest definition is merely a wish turned Godward.'

For further reading

Luke 11:1–13

Jesus told his disciples to pray to their *Father*, not to some distant authority figure. God is our Father who accepts us just as we are; and he wants us to come to him as ourselves, not as we think we ought to be. He already knows everything about us, so we don't have to wear a mask with him. Prayer is our opportunity to get to know him better, so it makes sense to spend time with him. We are to ask for 'our daily bread'. It is not a once-and-for-all prayer but one that we need to pray every day. God wants us to live each day of our lives in a prayerful relationship with him. In the verses that follow the Lord's Prayer, Jesus makes wonderful promises about the way God responds to our prayers. All we have to do is ask, seek, knock, and we will discover that God is waiting to pour out his blessings on us.

Prayer

Our Father in heaven, hallowed be your name. Your kingdom come, your will be done on earth as it is in heaven. Give us today our daily bread. Forgive us our debts, as we also have forgiven our debtors. And lead us not into temptation, but deliver us from the evil one. For yours is the kingdom, the power and the glory, for ever and ever. Amen.

Signs of civilization

Written a few days after the murder of London headteacher, Philip Lawrence, in 1995.

Finally, brothers, whatever is true, whatever is noble, whatever is right, whatever is pure, whatever is lovely, whatever is admirable—if anything is excellent or praiseworthy—think about such things.
PHILIPPIANS 4:8

The murder of headteacher Philip Lawrence has prompted much public comment this week. Surely the most eloquent came from his widow, Frances, who wrote an open letter to the 440 students of St George's Catholic School. In a dignified and moving letter, she spoke of her husband's many qualities as a man, and concluded with these words:

Violence is not a knife in the hand. It grows like a poison tree inside people who, unlike yourselves, have not learned to value other human beings. Now I trust you to work as hard as you can, in school and at home, to create a world in which goodness is never again destroyed by evil.

Frances Lawrence is right in reminding us of the responsibility we all share in refusing to allow prejudice, anger, jealousy, hatred and pride to grow unchecked. And the uprooting of such destructive attitudes begins with ourselves—not Parliament or police officers.

A few days ago a restaurant manager told me how her staff dreaded Christmas. 'Everyone is so rude and short-tempered, they treat you like dirt,' she said. So much for the season of peace on earth and goodwill towards men.

Anthropologist Margaret Meade was once asked by a student for the earliest sign of civilization in a given culture. You might suppose the answer would have been an agricultural tool or a piece of simple art. If so, you'd be wrong. Meade's reply was: 'A healed femur.' She pointed out that no healed femurs were found where the law of the jungle ruled; there it was a case of the survival of the fittest. But a healed femur showed that someone cared enough to hunt, cook and care for that injured person— until they were well enough to fend for themselves.

Compassion is the first sign of civilization. A caring society is a civilized society. And compassion goes beyond coughing up a few quid for Children in Need or the Salvation Army—deserving causes though they both are.

Compassion, in part at least, is seen in the everyday way we deal with a waitress or a headteacher, and how we teach our children to treat them too.

For further reading

ISAIAH 58:1–14

Do you ever find yourself saying, 'I give to this charity' or 'I do my bit for others'? We try to compensate for what we don't do with the things that we do do. Isaiah 58 describes how the Israelites tried to compensate for the exploitation of their workers and for their quarrelling and strife by outward religious observance. God, of course, saw right through them. Because they were not living each day trying to serve him, their occasional fasting was worthless. Romans 3:23 tells us that 'all have sinned and fall short of the glory of God'. We can never do enough to excuse our failings and to earn God's love but we can seek to live consistent lives, not expecting God to overlook our sins because we have put large sums of money in the church offering or because we never miss church on Sunday. Everything we can do for God is a thank offering in gratitude for his undeserved love shown to us.

Prayer

Take my life, and let it be
Consecrated, Lord, to Thee;
Take my moments and my days,
Let them flow in ceaseless praise.
FRANCES RIDLEY HAVERGAL (1836–79)

Wise warnings

Whatever you have learned or received or heard from me, or seen in me—put it into practice. And the God of peace will be with you.
PHILIPPIANS 4:9

Have you noticed how many products now come complete with detailed warnings and disclaimers? I suspect it's a by-product of increased compensation claims by consumers chasing their rights. But warning labels seem to have reached a silly high-point.

An American-based group now presents annual awards for the most ridiculous warnings, and recently announced their 1998 prizes. First place went to a baby-stroller bearing the stern command, 'Remove your child before folding'. Second prize went to a print cartridge bearing the inscription, 'Do not eat toner', and third place for a firelighter declaring, 'Do not use near fire'.

Now before you say, 'It could never happen here', be warned—the disease is spreading. A well-known supermarket chain sells a tiramisu dessert which carries the advice, 'Do not turn upside down', while Britain's favourite high street shop sells a bread and butter pudding which warns, 'Take care—product will be hot after heating'. And a leading chemist has a cough syrup for young children that states, 'Do not drive car or operate machinery. Avoid alcoholic drinks.'

For all the reasoning behind such warnings, I wonder if treating people like complete idiots is counter-productive. Personally, whenever I spot a Sybil Fawlty lecture coming on, it brings out the Basil in me.

But warnings are important. From our first tottering steps, friendly suggestions such as 'Watch out' and 'Don't touch' usually provide good advice. Experience teaches that the way to tell wise warnings from pointless ones is to look at who is doing the talking. If it's a parent who loves you, a friend that cares, or a teacher you trust, the warning is usually worth heeding. But if it comes from a cynic who would love to see you fall flat on your face, you have every reason to doubt their motives.

This helps me to make sense of the warnings God lays down in the Bible, touching such important issues as money, sex, friendship, recreation and what occupies our minds and hearts.

Forget the caricatures; this is no nanny deity intent on nagging us through life, desperate to see us fail so that another load of guilt can be heaped on us. This is a loving Father who longs for prodigals to wake up, come home and get a life.

Warnings that come from the One who is not dying to know us—but died to know us—are rooted in love.

For further reading

PHILIPPIANS 4:4–13

We are wise if we fill our minds with thoughts of what is true, noble, right, pure, lovely and admirable because this will influence what we say and how we act. Paul follows his exhortation in Philippians to fill our minds with what is 'excellent or praiseworthy' (v. 8) with the words, 'Whatever you have learned or received or heard from me, or seen in me—put it into practice' (v. 9). It's often said that actions speak louder than words. The way we live our lives usually says a lot more about us than the words that come out of our mouths, and it is true that how we act can demonstrate the sincerity or otherwise of what we say. The question is, are our lives an example to follow or a warning of what to avoid? Paul was able to hold himself up as an example of what pleases God. Can we do the same?

Prayer

Grant, heavenly Father, that the sermon preached by my life might be pleasing to you and an example to others.

Jesus visits the spin doctor

Written a few days after the 1997 General Election.

Folly delights a man who lacks judgment, but a man of understanding keeps a straight course.

PROVERBS 15:21

With the General Election out of the way, I can now share a secret report that has fallen into my hands, entitled, 'Jesus visits the spin doctor'.

Let me start by saying that you have quite a bit going for you, but the total package needs brightening up. For example, the Messiah thing really connects —everyone's looking for a new star to follow, but we've detected elements of negative positioning in your campaign.

First, the people you hang out with. The 'working class lad from the suburbs' image is useful in attracting a few voters, but tax collectors and prostitutes do nothing to increase public confidence. Ditch them and cultivate high-powered friends instead.

Second, we notice you write your own speeches—some nice touches too. I like the bit about 'taking the plank out of your own eye before trying to remove the speck in your brother's eye'. But a lot of your material is rough around the edges. I mean, 'It is easier for a camel to go through the eye of a needle than for a rich man to enter the Kingdom of God' won't go down well if you drive a BMW and have a villa in Marbella, will it? We have a team who can help— I've got a hunch there could be a book in all of this—a big one too, if you play your cards right!

Another thing is this business about the cost of being a disciple. Our focus groups have fed back that they don't like it. We have a motto: 'Play up the benefits and keep the costs hidden.' Works well with insurance companies and political parties, so I don't see why a potential Messiah shouldn't try it for size.

Keep promising the world and give all this 'take up your cross and follow me' bit a miss.

That brings me to the last point—death.

Sorry to say it, but you're obsessed with the subject and it's a very negative image. I mean, have you seen a crucifixion? Opinion polls indicate that no one will vote for a man who says he is going to be crucified. There's a chance of a small sympathy vote—but the masses won't buy a dead Messiah...

Unless, of course, you had any plans for a comeback... now that would be original...

For further reading

LUKE 14:25–35

Jesus told the truth. In this passage he was on the way to Jerusalem and the cross and he set out the costs of being a follower of his very starkly. His first concern was not how his hearers would receive what he said. He did not mislead them to gain popularity. He wanted them and us to realize that there would be a price to pay in being his disciple. He did not want thoughtless followers who would begin to follow him and then fall by the wayside when things got tough. When we present Christianity and ourselves as Christians to others, we may be tempted to put a more attractive 'spin' on things but the bottom line is that we are forgiven sinners. Our responsibility in sharing our faith with others is to be honest about Christianity and our own failures and to let God worry about the result.

Prayer

Lord, make me a person whose first desire is to speak truthfully even when this may make me unpopular.

Playing our part

What good is it, my brothers, if a man claims to have faith but has no deeds?

JAMES 2:14

A notice outside a Plymouth church caught my eye the other morning. A bright dayglo poster declared, 'This church is full of hypocrites', then in small print underneath: 'We can always move up and make room for one more!'

Hypocrisy is something we all hate and find so easy to spot—at least in others. We readily identify with Mark Twain's observation: 'He was a good man in the worst sense of the term.'

The word 'hypocrite' came into the English language from Ancient Greek but in those days it didn't carry such a negative meaning. A *hupokrites* was an actor, a speechmaker or someone who interpreted dreams. It came to mean someone who played a part or put on an act. It's easy to understand how it was used to describe a person who said one thing but did another.

Churches don't have a monopoly on hypocrisy, although I grant you that religion breeds a particularly nasty type of the disease. We are all guilty of it whenever we reach the credibility gap that exists between our claims and our character.

Jesus, in the Sermon on the Mount, warns of the danger of good things—such as giving to others, prayer and fasting—becoming empty showmanship, devoid of real worth.

All of us need reminding that it's actions rather than acting that break down the walls of hypocrisy we all build around us from time to time.

I sometimes turn to this solemn reminder—a poem written by a homeless woman who turned to a vicar for help and found none. She handed it to a regional officer for the charity, Shelter:

I was hungry,
and you formed a humanities group to discuss my hunger.
I was imprisoned,
and you crept off quietly to your chapel and prayed for my release.
I was naked,
and in your mind you debated the morality of my appearance.
I was sick,
and you knelt and thanked God for your health.
I was homeless,
and you preached to me of the spiritual shelter of the love of God,
I was lonely,
and you left me alone to pray for me.
You seem so holy, so close to God.
But I am still very hungry—and lonely—and cold.

QUOTED BY JOHN STOTT IN *ISSUES FACING CHRISTIANS TODAY*, MARSHALL PICKERING, 1990

For further reading

MATTHEW 25:31–46

Sometimes the enormity of the world's needs overwhelms us. We feel powerless to make any difference. We wonder: what's the point of even trying? Jesus said, 'The poor you will always have with you' (Matthew 26:11). He recognized that, in our fallen, sinful world, where the greedy take the lion's share, there will always be poverty; there is nothing we can do to abolish it completely. But we are called to make a difference where we can. If we look around us there are many opportunities to help others—by giving financially or practically, by writing a letter, by encouraging those working 'on the front line' and, above all, by praying. We should keep our eyes open for the opportunity to make a little difference, even if it only scratches the surface of the need, because although it may seem only a small thing, Jesus says that we are doing it not only for him but to him.

Prayer

Ask God to open your eyes to the opportunities around you to help others. Pray that he will increase the little that you are able to do so that it will make a big difference to others and that he will accept it as your offering to him.

Windows on Church

The upward look

Let us not give up meeting together, as some are in the habit of doing, but let us encourage one another—and all the more as you see the Day approaching.

HEBREWS 10:25

If I had to pick the three most frequently asked questions in my job, one of them must be: 'Do you have to go to church to be a Christian?' The short answer is no. Equally, you can spend your life kicking a football alone—but if you want to get the most out of the sport you'll soon discover it's a game best played with others.

But what's the point of going to church? One New Testament letter contains a rather curious statement on the subject: 'Let us not give up meeting together, as some are in the habit of doing, but let us encourage one another—and all the more as you see the Day approaching.'

It seems that some of the early followers of Jesus lost their first flush of enthusiasm and had opted out of meeting with other Christians for worship and teaching. There may have been several things that caused this—but whatever their excuse, neglecting being together as 'church' was having a harmful effect.

Over the next few studies I intend to set out several basic reasons why church attendance can be good for our spiritual health. There's another motive behind this, which I will let you know in due course. For now, the first reason is—quite simply—we need an upward look.

Our Creator designed life with rhythm. Our bodies need a certain amount of sleep within the 24-hour pattern and most of us recognize the benefit of time off from everyday pressures. That is why God set apart one day in the week for renewal. The Sabbath principle—one day in seven for rest—was not designed to get people into church but to allow us time for space, reflection and worship.

One day set aside for family, for friends, for leisure, sounds like an EC directive that most of us would go along with. But there is a vital ingredient missing from the mix—God.

I go to church on Sunday to get a bigger glimpse of God and a smaller perception of myself. It is a time for putting the universe back into a proper perspective. We need time for prayer, for listening and for worship.

Albert Schweitzer wrote, 'Do not let Sunday be taken from you. If your soul has no Sunday it becomes an orphan.' Whoever we are, we can all benefit from a regular upward look.

For further reading

PSALM 100:1–5

Sometimes our attitude seems to be that going to church is a duty we owe to God, rather than a privilege that we have been *given* to enjoy. This psalm puts going to worship God in its proper perspective. We are to worship gladly, not grudgingly. We are only a small part of God's worshipping creation in 'all the earth' (v. 1) with whom we are able to join together in spirit, wherever we are, whatever our circumstances, to 'shout for joy to the Lord' (v. 1). Not only is our worship a contribution to the global worship of God but it is joined to that of past generations and those still to come because God's 'love endures for ever; his faithfulness continues through all generations' (v. 5). If 'we are his people, the sheep of his pasture' (v. 3), we shouldn't miss this opportunity to 'enter his gates with thanksgiving' (v. 4).

Prayer

Forgive me, Lord, if I sometimes have a 'take it or leave it' attitude to meeting with others to worship you. Help me to take advantage of my freedom to be a part of your Church openly and without fear.

The inward look

For all have sinned and fall short of the glory of God.

ROMANS 3:23

My car failed its MoT last week. The mechanic gave a sigh that is the practised art of workmen everywhere. I interpreted this to mean, 'This is going to cost a bomb to put right, so brace yourself.' I was right.

'Why bother with church?' is a question I began to answer in the last reading. One reason is the *upward look*—we are called to worship God. A second reason could be described as the *inward look*. And this is where my failed MoT comes in.

My car was checked, and failed—in several areas—to meet the requirements. One reason for going to church is to listen to God's voice, to check and adjust our lives in line with what he says. It provides a rare opportunity in a busy week to stop, listen and think.

Looking inwards is not an excuse for ignoring needs around us—far from it. If we listen hard to God, we pick up his deep compassion for a hurt world. As Dorothy L. Sayers put it, 'When we come home like the Prodigal Son, God sends us out again as the Good Samaritan.'

I visited a church last Sunday. It was not a church in my denomination, but I discovered long ago that God is not so much bothered by the label on the door as with the contents inside. Almost four hundred people met for worship, many of them young families. There came a sense of God in the service and the minister took an unplanned step. He called for a time of silence. Some stood, some sat, a few knelt and, for fifteen minutes, the congregation bathed in the presence of God.

Human beings have an ability to take an art form and turn it into a science. Some would want to build an 'altar' or ceremony on the basis of such an experience. Some would establish a new denomination called

'The Church of the Fifteen Minutes Silence'. Such foolishness obscures the real point.

Of course, I can hear God by myself. but I need to beware of the arrogance of isolation. He speaks to his gathered people—wherever they may be.

The philosopher Francis Schaeffer entitled one of his many books about God, *He is there and he is not silent* (IVP).

Going to church is, in part, about tuning in to our talkative God.

For further reading

HEBREWS 10:1–14; 1 JOHN 1:8–10

According to Old Testament law, the animal sacrifices had to be made year after year as a 'reminder of sins'. They did not deal once and for all with the intrinsic problem of sin. But Jesus' death broke that cycle and paid the price for sin for all time, past, present and future. As Hebrews 10:12 says, 'When this priest had offered for all time one sacrifice for sins, he sat down at the right hand of God.' God's justice has been satisfied and sin need no longer rule over us, but we are still so prone to take for granted what God has done, and to make compromises with the world during the week, that we need a day to focus especially on God and to get back on track. And joining with others in an act of worship away from other distractions provides a valuable opportunity to hear what God wants to say to us.

Prayer

Though I forget him, and wander away,
Still he doth love me wherever I stray;
Back to his dear loving arms will I flee
When I remember that Jesus loves me.
PHILIP P. BLISS (1838–76)

The sideways look

And let us consider how we may spur one another on towards love and good deeds.
HEBREWS 10:24

The following appeared on the small ads board of a corner shop:

LOST. Dog with three legs, blind in one eye, missing right ear, tail broken and recently castrated. Answers to the name of 'Lucky'.

You may be wondering about the link between a sad dog and my answer to the question, 'Why bother with church?' Being part of a church provides an *upward look* and an *inward look*. It also opens the way for a *sideways look*, and this is where 'Lucky' comes in.

I once visited an ancient church building and noticed large brass rails running above the pews. I was told that curtains were once hung from them, so that other worshippers would not distract people. Those wealthy enough to rent a family pew felt they deserved some privacy in church.

I can't imagine anything further from the New Testament understanding of what it means to be church. Church is meant to be a place of friendship and relationship, a place where barriers of class, gender, age, colour and culture are crossed, almost unnoticeably. It is a place where love and support can be offered and received. The first Christians used a word to sum all this up—*koinonia*—which is translated as 'fellowship'. It means quite literally 'sharingship'. That is what makes sense of such statements as, 'Let us consider how we may spur one another on to love and good deeds'.

Going to a church building is about meeting with God—it is also about meeting with others. Churches that grow discover that fellowship means more than a limp handshake and a weak cup of tea. It is about opening our eyes—and our hearts—to people who sit around us.

Lucky was a dog who didn't live up to his name. His catalogue of injuries was plain for all to see. But sitting next to you at church could be a broken person whose wounds are not that obvious. God's care for them will not float down from the sky; it will come through hands like yours or mine.

If I go to church to suit myself, I come away disappointed. But when I go to church and take a sideways look, I am enriched. Go to church with your eyes open and you'll see what I mean.

As they say, 'A cold church is like cold butter. Neither spreads well.'

For further reading

MARK 10:46–52; LUKE 19:1–10

There were times in Jesus' ministry when the disciples or the crowds tried to prevent people coming to Jesus. They didn't want him to be bothered by small children or a blind beggar or a social outcast. Perhaps the crowd deliberately closed ranks against Zacchaeus, the short, unpopular tax collector. Thankfully, Jesus looked with different eyes and saw the potential along with the need in all those who approached him. How encouraging that is for us. And what an example of how we should treat others. The notion that some people are more important than others has always been prevalent in the world and it's easy to go along with it unthinkingly; we are drawn to mix with people who seem to be like us; but we have been called to follow the One who 'came to seek and to save what was lost' (Luke 19:10). However 'respectable' we may be, at heart we are *all* the same and Jesus wants to meet with us.

Prayer

Lord, help me to look with your eyes of compassion as you have looked at me. Thank you that you 'came to seek and to save what was lost', including me.

The backwards look

For whenever you eat this bread and drink this cup, you proclaim the Lord's death until he comes.

1 CORINTHIANS 11:26

I only met him two weeks ago. He introduced himself as a former naval officer who had taken the big step into civvy street, landing a job with a large engineering company. This coincided with his decision to marry and start a family.

When the first baby arrived, he and his wife approached the parish church to arrange a christening. They were invited to join a special preparation class, led by the vicar.

The couple were impressed by the welcome and sincerity of others in the group and within a few weeks began to attend morning service. In his own words, they were 'blown away' by what they found. A packed church with dozens of young families, a service led in language they could understand, preaching that was relevant and a genuine sense that people were interested in them—they even remembered their names.

Within a few short months the couple had come to a personal faith and went ahead with the baptism of their child, understanding and meaning their solemn vows. I asked what had convinced them about the Christian faith. He explained that, being an engineer, he had a mind that needed to understand how things fitted together and, most of all, what made them work.

Over the months he had come to realize that this faith was built on fact, not fiction. Jesus of Nazareth was not from the pages of legend—but solid, reliable history. The more he listened and then went away to check out the facts, the more convinced he became.

Why bother with church? As well as an upward, inward and sideways look, it offers an opportunity for something else—a *backwards look*. We are reminded of a God who has acted in history—supremely in the life of Jesus. When scripture is read, it tells of God's actions. When prayers are offered, they point to his involvement. Each time bread and wine are shared, we are reminded: 'Christ has died. Christ is risen. Christ shall come again.'

My memory is so bad, I need a regular backward look, in order to remember with love and gratitude the one who 'paid a debt he did not owe, because I owed a debt I could not pay'.

And as my new friend reminded me, this sort of backward look is not a time for sentimental reflection, rather a challenge to act on the facts.

For further reading

EXODUS 13:1–16

The ceremonies and feasts laid down in the Old Testament weren't just times for thanksgiving and celebration but ways of building into the nation's life reminders of where the Israelites had come from and how God had delivered them. They were also a way of passing on truths to subsequent generations. At the Last Supper, Jesus instigated an act of remembrance for us that not only looks back to his death on the cross but at the same time looks forward to the culmination of that event, when Jesus will return in all his majesty. We look backwards not in order to live in the past but as a springboard for living today and in anticipation of our glorious future. Our trustworthy God, who has performed marvellous acts in the past, has even greater things in store for us.

Prayer

When we look back, Lord, to what you have done for us, we are overwhelmed that you should care so much that you were prepared to die for us. Help us to look back often to that fact in history as we seek to serve you every day.

The forward look

Written after England Coach, Glenn Hoddle, dropped star player, Paul Gascoigne, in the run-up to the 1998 World Cup Finals.

I press on towards the goal to win the prize for which God has called me heavenwards in Christ Jesus.

PHILIPPIANS 3:14

Well, should he or shouldn't he? That is the question. There may be an earthquake in Afghanistan and continued famine in Sudan, but let's get our priorities right. Here's the really important news item—should Hoddle have dropped Gazza?

Forgive the cynicism, especially as it comes from a passionate football supporter like me, but every now and then I come to the conclusion that the tabloid culture of 'Cool Britannia' needs to be put to sleep quickly and quietly.

In this section I have been answering the question, 'Why bother with church?' We have talked about the upward, inward, sideways and backward look. Today it's about the *forward look*, and Glenn Hoddle's controversial decision provides an illustration.

The England coach faced a tough choice but, in the end, Gascoigne's lack of fitness ruled him out for selection. Hoddle looked ahead to a punishing schedule of games and reluctantly realized that, for all his talent, Gazza would be a liability rather than an asset. It was a choice not made on the basis of sentiment or with an eye to popularity ratings. It was cool and calculated and based on a vision of what was needed in the future.

Some people use church as a means of escape and, whilst I have some sympathy for those seeking shelter from the storm, it is not the primary reason Christ calls his people together. Worship, prayer, scripture, teaching and friendship are meant to point us forward. Take the service of Communion, for example. Those familiar words from the New Testament that are often read include a pregnant phrase: '...until he comes...' (1 Corinthians 11:26).

That's the forward look—a reminder that history has a purpose and a goal, that one day God will write the final full stop on the last page of history. Jesus is coming back!

Pentecost is the time when the Church remembers the coming of the Holy Spirit on a bunch of ordinary people who went out and turned their world upside down. They lived with a focus and energy that the Church has rarely seen since. Why? Because they believed time was running out and that gave urgency to their mission.

Believe it or not, church is meant to do the same for us. Far from escape, it reminds us what reality looks like. As Hoddle found out, it faces us with tough choices.

Tomorrow's vision sharpens today's decisions.

For further reading

PHILIPPIANS 3:12—4:1
It has become less fashionable to regard Sunday as the first day of the week, but if we see it in that light it helps us to be forward-looking. Being in church on a Sunday gives us an opportunity to forget 'what is behind' (3:13) (the forgiven failures and omissions of the previous week) and restore our energy to 'press on towards the goal to win the prize...' (3:14). We can regain our eternal perspective as we are reminded that 'our citizenship is in heaven' and face the coming week with a new sense of urgency as we affirm that we are eagerly awaiting the return of our Saviour. We are encouraged in our faith by joining with like-minded people, not in order to escape from reality but so that we might see more clearly the needs of the Christless community in which we live and work.

Prayer

Help me, Lord, not to lose my eternal perspective as I go about my everyday life. Teach me to see the eternal significance of the mundane.

The outward look

The fruit of the righteous is a tree of life, and he who wins souls is wise.

PROVERBS 11:30

A harassed mum shouts up the stairs, 'This is the last time I'm calling. We'll be late for church—get up!'

A plaintive voice floats from under the duvet: 'I don't want to go. I don't like church. No one talks to me and it's boring.'

Mum retorts, 'I am not discussing that with you—get cracking.'

'Give me three good reasons why I should go,' says the muffled voice.

'OK,' says Mum. 'Number one, the service starts in fifteen minutes. Number two, you're 47 years of age. Number three, you're the vicar. Now move it.'

'Why bother with church?' is a question I have posed in this section. And I have tried to answer it by revealing the upward, inward, sideways, backward and forward look it provides. There is one more: the *outward look*.

A year or so ago, I spent a couple of months travelling the motorways of Britain, investigating why some churches grow and others decline, as part of an academic research project.

I studied five growing congregations in different parts of the country. They all belonged to different denominations and had their own flavour and appeal.

The research uncovered some fascinating things but one is worth mentioning in connection with the outward look. In compiling some detailed survey material, we asked a question along the lines: 'What do you think your church should be doing better?' The overwhelming response fell in two categories: (1) doing more in our community; and (2) doing more to share our faith with those outside church.

These were growing churches—one, for example, had gone from seventeen members to 500 plus in just sixteen years. Perhaps a clue to their growth was seen in their desire to be doing more for those outside. It was Archbishop William Temple who often said that the Church is the only body that exists solely for the benefit of its non-members. That should be written in letters ten feet high over every church and chapel door in Britain.

It seems significant that churches that grow are those that have an eye on others rather than themselves. But then we don't need a research project to tell us that. The idea of self-giving rather than self-serving lies at the heart of the teaching of Jesus.

The challenge facing the Church in this new millennium is, in short, less of self and more of others.

For further reading

JONAH 3:1—4:11

From beginning to end, the book of Jonah describes a man who wants to wriggle out of obeying God's command to go and do something for others. In chapter 1 verse 9 Jonah's words tell us that he did not neglect to worship God or declare to others his commitment to him. Verse 12 shows us a man with a conscience and Jonah's prayer inside the fish demonstrates his deep faith. Yet when it came to going to preach to the people of Nineveh, Jonah was more than reluctant and when they responded to his message he was dismayed. He did not share God's concern for them, but God gave Jonah a living lesson about his all-encompassing love for all people. The Bible doesn't tell us how Jonah received that lesson, but what about us? Is God asking us to reach out to someone we find hard to love, to go into a situation we find hostile and threatening?

Prayer

Lord, soften my heart towards all those you love. Help me to go willingly wherever you may send me, knowing that you have already prepared the way.

Windows on Wisdom

Clearing out the garage

Written in August 1995 at the time of commemorative services for Victory over Japan.

'Shouldn't you have had mercy on your fellow-servant just as I had on you?'
MATTHEW 18:33

It was the summer of 1960 and Vera and Colin Lowther had just taken delivery of their new car, a Chevrolet Stylemaster, specially imported from the USA. To celebrate, they packed a picnic hamper, climbed into the gleaming black saloon and headed for the Derbyshire countryside.

It had been a perfect day up until the moment they arrived back at their Sheffield home. Colin Lowther suddenly collapsed with a massive heart attack and died. He was 45 years old.

Vera suffered inconsolable grief; she lost interest in life and became withdrawn, only venturing out to the shops, her main company being her dog and cat.

She left the Chevrolet in the garage where Colin had parked it the night he died. She rejected all suggestions of selling it. Kind and concerned family members urged her to begin a new life, but Vera simply couldn't get over the loss of her husband.

Vera died last year at eighty years of age. They hacked through the undergrowth blocking the driveway and opened the garage door. The Chevrolet was rolled out into the sunlight for the first time in 34 years. In the boot was the picnic hamper, untouched since that memorable, tragic, final outing.

It is understandable when we want to hold on to things from the past but it isn't always helpful.

The moving photos of ex-Allied and Japanese servicemen attending commemorative services this week has brought some haunting memories for those who still carry scars. Talk of forgiveness has been in the air—and also of the importance of publicly acknowledging guilt and doing something practical to demonstrate genuine remorse.

But like Vera Lowther, some of us find it hard to clear the garage. We store away hurt, resentment, anger, rejection and things we've tried to hide from ourselves as much as anyone.

When Alexander Pope wrote, 'To err is human, to forgive divine,' he declared a profound truth.

We need help beyond ourselves if we are going to clear some of the things that make us live as prisoners of the past.

As Jesus taught us to pray: 'Forgive us our sins, for we also forgive everyone who sins against us' (Luke 11:4).

For further reading

MATTHEW 18:15–35

This passage gives clear guidance on how we are to deal with those who have sinned against us: we are to do all in our power, including enlisting the help of others, to resolve the matter. It's interesting that the onus is on the one who has been hurt to take the initiative in restoring the relationship. When it comes to forgiveness, we are not to look at what the other person has done to us but at what God has done for us. The emphasis in this passage is not on how we feel (hurt, offended) but on what we must do (make the first move towards reconciliation). We need an altered perspective. And because of the way God has made us, once we start to obey him we will find that it is much easier to let go of our own 'rights' than to hold a grudge or seek to pay someone back. The consequences for us if we do not do this, or for the other person if he or she refuses to listen, are very sobering.

Prayer

Ask God to show you if there is any 'unfinished business' in your life. Ask for his help in summoning up the courage to begin to put things right.

Serving hands

You yourselves know that these hands of mine have supplied my own needs and the needs of my companions.
ACTS 20:34

Albrecht Dürer's *Praying Hands* is one of the world's most famous religious pictures. The etching dates back to the fifteenth century and has been reproduced in many forms.

There is a story behind its creation, concerning Dürer and a close friend called Franz. The two lived and worked together, training as artists in their spare time. Both had the ambition to become painters but realized they could never afford full-time tuition.

The friends eventually decided that Franz would concentrate on working, in order to support Dürer as he trained. They agreed that, when money was available, Franz could start his studies as well. After some years, Albrecht Dürer became successful enough as an artist to repay his friend's kindness. It was Franz's turn to go to art school.

Sadly, Franz's hands had become so damaged through heavy manual work that there was no chance of him using them to pursue a serious career as an artist. His years of hard work to support his friend had cost him his dream.

Dürer used his friend's worn hands as a model for his famous etching. I suppose, in part, it was tribute to the one who gave up his own ambition in order to serve a friend.

I can never look at that picture in the same way again. I had always viewed it as a symbol of prayer and devotion to God, but I now see it in a different light. It is an image that teaches that sacrifice and service lie at the heart of true prayer.

As I write these words, I am about to embark on a trip to the other side of the world, visiting a group of Christians who devote their lives to serving others in their community, regardless of colour, status or beliefs. Through a host of programmes, they are working with the poor and oppressed, putting the love of Christ into action through words and deeds.

Although I always look forward to being with them, I find it a disturbing time. The way they live and serve challenges my comfortable faith and easy lifestyle. They put my petty moans into perspective by their sacrificial service and they undermine my prejudice by their unconditional love.

Like Franz's hands, they remind me that when we pray for others we may well be the means of answering our own prayers.

Praying hands, you see, should be serving hands.

For further reading

ACTS 9:36–42

Dorcas was a Christian who served with her hands. She was known for her good works and was a much-valued member of the Christian community in Joppa, with a practical concern for the poor, perhaps in particular for the widows mentioned in the story. When she died, two men from the fellowship there were sent to Peter, who they had heard was nearby in Lydda. Peter came back with them and, by God's power, brought Dorcas back to life. It is because of this that we learn a little of the story of a woman who served God in many small and unremarkable ways. Because of the miracle that happened to her, 'many people believed in the Lord' (v. 42). Dorcas' faithfulness in serving others led to much greater fruit than anyone could ever have anticipated. Every act of service to God is worth doing, however insignificant.

Prayer

Take my hands, and let them move
At the impulse of thy love;
Take my feet, and let them be
Swift and beautiful for thee.
FRANCES RIDLEY HAVERGAL (1836–79)

Second chances

This day I call heaven and earth as witnesses against you that I have set before you life and death, blessings and curses. Now choose life, so that you and your children may live and that you may love the Lord your God, listen to his voice, and hold fast to him.

DEUTERONOMY 30:19–20

The police officer already had enough on his plate when the emergency call came in. A blizzard was blowing full force, creating chaos all over town, when news arrived of a fire in an apartment block.

Officer MacGuinness and his partner arrived at the scene, waded through waist-high snow and carried two little boys out of the burning building to safety. Both boys, one aged eighteen months and the other three years old, were badly burned. By some miracle they both survived, although it was a close thing and both needed several years of skin grafts.

Walter MacGuinness kept an interest in the boys' progress, and their thankful father brought them to the police station from time to time as a mark of his gratitude to the officers whose bravery saved their lives, and to show how well they were recovering.

A few years ago, Walter MacGuinness faced one of the toughest days in his police career. He sat in a court in Massachusetts recalling the night he carried the unconscious baby boy out of the blazing building. He now had to watch as the man whom the boy had grown to be was sentenced to one and a half years in prison for assaulting an elderly woman and attacking his own girlfriend.

Eighteen years on from the night he rescued the toddler from the flames, Officer MacGuinness arrested and charged the man whose life he had saved.

Wilfredo Rivera, who as a toddler had been rescued from the fire, claims to have no recollection of MacGuinness or of his father taking him to the police station as a youngster. But MacGuinness recalls it all too well and describes recent events as 'a twist of fate'. He added, 'I did what I had to do in 1978 and I did what I had to do today.'

How sad that a life that was saved ended up being wasted, at least, until now. The Christian leader, Paul, was well aware that people who claimed to be followers of Christ could end up living in a way that fell short of God's standards. His words are worth recalling: 'Do not let sin reign in your mortal body... offer yourselves to God, as those who have been brought from death to life' (Romans 6:12–13).

In other words, live as people who have been rescued—and never forget what you have been rescued from.

For further reading

2 SAMUEL 14:21–33

2 Samuel 13—18 tells the story of King David's son, Absalom. He appeared to have every advantage as he grew up in the royal family, but he was a ruthless man. Even after he had taken revenge on his brother by murdering him, David forgave Absalom and had him brought back from exile. Absalom was given a second chance, but instead of taking advantage of this opportunity to reform, he used it to betray his father and this, ultimately, led to his premature and unpleasant death. These chapters make tragic reading. Absalom chose the evil way and paid the price. God has given us a 'second chance' through Jesus' death on the cross. We should be careful to live a life that honours God and seeks his way, bearing in mind that all our choices have consequences.

Prayer

Lord, so often in the past I have needed not just a second chance but a third and a fourth... Thank you for your patience and mercy to me when I have made the wrong choices. Help me to learn to choose and act wisely.

Who's in charge?

'Lord, teach us to pray.'
LUKE 11:1

Winter-time flu seems to be as annual a British event as the Grand National! If nothing else, I suppose a week of coughing and feeling miserable about life at least reminds us that the good health that most of us enjoy should never be taken for granted.

Ben Patterson was a minister of a busy church in America when he was suddenly confined to bed for six weeks. A serious problem with his spine forced him to lie flat on his back with a minimum of movement. He openly confesses that he was not a patient patient. One day, out of sheer boredom, he asked his wife to let him have the directory of church members, and began to pray systematically for each individual connected with the congregation. For two or three hours a day he prayed for people and discovered, in turn, how much his own life was enriched.

As he prepared to return to work, he recognized that he would not have the same opportunity to spend time praying for others. Patterson reports, 'God spoke to me very clearly. "You have the same twenty-four hours each day when you're weak as when you're strong. The only difference is that when you're strong you think you're in charge. When you're weak you know you aren't."'

It was a priceless lesson to learn, even if it was a hard way to learn it. I freely admit that a severe bout of flu often makes you want to crawl away and forget the world. But I was challenged by Patterson's example of turning a bad situation into something good and useful.

A few years ago, a book with an unlikely title shot to the top of the religious bestseller lists. It was called *Don't Just Stand There—Pray Something!* Its author, Ron Dunn, wrote it out of personal experience of discovering the power of prayer. The fact that it achieved such high worldwide sales perhaps indicates that many people believed it was a topic where they needed help.

The disciples of Jesus identified with that need when they asked him, 'Lord, teach us to pray'.

I hope it doesn't take a dose of flu to make us realize how important that request may prove to be.

For further reading

JAMES 5:13–18; MATTHEW 6:5–13

What greater encouragement could we have to persevere in our praying than James' comment that 'Elijah was a man just like us' (James 5:17)? Elijah saw incredible, miraculous answers to some of his prayers but this was because he was praying to our great and powerful God, not because he was some kind of 'super' man of God. Not only is God almighty and able to answer our prayers but, as Jesus describes him, he is 'our Father' (Matthew 6:9). As his children, we come to a loving Father who delights in us. As we embark on a lifetime's journey of prayer, he welcomes us. He would much rather we came faltering and stumbling over our requests and praise than not at all. There is no reason why we should not pray and every reason why we should.

Prayer

I thank you, Almighty Father, that you are always made glad when I pray, however inarticulate or hesitant my prayers are.

Success stories?

Whoever loves money never has money enough; whoever loves wealth is never satisfied with his income.

ECCLESIASTES 5:10

Most of us struggle with money—or, to be more accurate, the lack of it. It is hard not to believe that if our money worries were solved, life would be so much easier. But would it? Not according to an article I read recently.

In 1932 a group of the world's most successful financiers met at the Edgewater Beach Hotel in Chicago. Present were:

- the President of the largest independent steel company in the USA
- the greatest wheat speculator
- the President of the New York Stock Exchange
- a member of the President's Cabinet
- the greatest 'bear' (trader) on Wall Street
- the President of the Bank of International Settlements
- the head of the world's greatest monopoly

Collectively, these tycoons controlled more wealth than there was in the United States Treasury, and for years newspapers and magazines had been printing their success stories and urging the youth of the nation to follow their example.

Twenty-five years later, their stories were tragically different.

- The President of the largest steel company, Charles Schwab, lived on borrowed money for the last five years of his life and died penniless.
- The greatest wheat speculator, Arthur Cutten, died abroad, insolvent.
- The President of the New York Stock Exchange, Richard Whitney, had just been released from Sing Sing Prison.

- The member of the President's Cabinet, Albert Fall, was pardoned from prison so that he could die at home.
- The greatest 'bear' on Wall Street, Jesse Livermore, committed suicide.
- The President of the Bank of International Settlements, Leon Fraser, committed suicide.
- The head of the world's greatest monopoly, Ivar Kreugar, committed suicide.

The article concluded with this poignant remark: 'All of these men had learned how to make money but not one of them had learned how to live.'

Jesus was once invited to settle a squabble between relatives over an inheritance. He refused to get involved but instead made this startling reply: 'Be on your guard against all kinds of greed; a man's life does not consist in the abundance of his possessions' (Luke 12:15).

For further reading

HEBREWS 13:1–21

Among these verses of varied instructions on how to live we are told to keep our 'lives free from the love of money' (v. 5). It's possible to be deluded into thinking that money will bring us security but, as the verse in Ecclesiastes quoted above reminds us, once we start going after money we will always want more. The verses in Hebrews call us to be 'content with what you have' (v. 5), however much or little that may be. Our contentment should be based on God's promise: 'Never will I leave you; never will I forsake you' (v. 5). Worldly wealth is subject to all sorts of fluctuations and threats but God is completely dependable because 'Jesus Christ is the same yesterday and today and for ever' (v. 8). With our eyes fixed on him and his eternal priorities, we can begin to learn how to live.

Prayer

Thank you, Lord, that you are aware of our every need and that, if we make seeking your kingdom our priority, we do not need to spend time worrying about our material needs being met.

Investments and legacies

'You did not choose me, but I chose you and appointed you to go and bear fruit—fruit that will last.'
JOHN 15:16

Several years ago, a study was conducted among elderly people, all over 90 years of age. They were asked the question, 'If you could live your life again, what would you do differently?'

The survey revealed three main responses:

1. I would reflect more.
2. I would take more risks.
3. I would do more things that would live on after I'm dead.

Wise words which prove that hindsight gives you wisdom on the way down that you badly needed on the way up. But the thing that struck me about these people's replies was their desire to invest in a tomorrow they wouldn't see, to do more things that would live on after they were gone.

Not many of us will have the chance to leave millions of pounds to build a hospital or fight the war against world poverty, but there are richer legacies we can leave than those made up of cash. Think of some of the legacies we treasure most, and words like laughter, love, friendship and priceless memories come to mind. When my father died, he didn't leave me a penny. He couldn't because he didn't have any to leave. But the inheritance he passed on is made of more solid stuff than pounds and pence and stocks and shares. He left a legacy of faith that I saw lived out in a lifetime of serving others, a high regard for the Bible as God's living word and a deep devotion to Jesus Christ that, even in my most cynical years, I recognized as real. And I have never for a moment felt anything other than a wealthy man as far as my inheritance goes.

Louis Pasteur, the father of modern bacteriology, lived at a time when thousands died each year from rabies. He had worked for years to produce a vaccine and was about to begin experimenting on himself when a nine-year-old boy called Joseph Meister was bitten by a rabid dog. The boy's mother begged Pasteur for help and he injected Joseph for ten days—and the boy made a full recovery.

Years later, Pasteur requested three words to be engraved on his headstone: 'Joseph Meister lived.'

I know it sounds sombre but it's a question worth asking: what am I investing in today that will live on after I'm gone?

For further reading

2 KINGS 5:1–18

Despite her unenviable position as a slave, this young Israelite girl cared enough about the family with whom she lived to urge that Naaman should go to the prophet, Elisha, to ask for healing from his leprosy. Elisha might well have refused to help a foreigner and enemy of Israel but, fortunately for the girl, he didn't—and her concern for her master's physical well-being bore spiritual fruit in his life as well: 'Your servant will never again make burnt offerings and sacrifices to any other god but the Lord' (v. 17). We need to be alert to the underlying pain and spiritual hunger behind people's everyday conversation and have the courage to risk rebuff when we point them to the God who can heal their deepest hurts. In this way we can make eternal investments in other people's lives. We can follow the example of the slave girl whose name we do not know but whose story is still told today. God has called us not only to be different from the world but to make a difference in the world.

Prayer

Lord, I don't want to live selfishly and safely. I want to do things that will make a difference to people, and please you.

Damage below the waterline

Written at the launch of the movie *Titanic*.

Here is a trustworthy saying that deserves full acceptance: Christ
Jesus came into the world to save sinners—of whom I am the worst.
1 TIMOTHY 1:15

It is, without a doubt, a great film. I am immune to most forms of hype,
so the promotion which surrounded the launch of the movie, *Titanic*,
had put me in a mindset that expected to be disappointed. On the
contrary, I was stunned. It's a long time since I heard an audience
applaud loudly at the end of a film. (Bearing in mind that they had sat
for over three hours in a packed, hot auditorium, their applause was all
the more remarkable.)

The big screen brings home the enormity of the disaster that sank the
ship they called unsinkable. Fifteen hundred people lost their lives on
the vessel's maiden voyage to New York in 1912. At the time, Titanic
was regarded as an opulent testimony to people's ability to tame the
seas.

Recent discovery of the wreckage has prompted intensive
investigations. Divers and scientists used modern technology to probe
the wreck as it lay buried in mud under three miles of ocean. Their
investigations caused the widely accepted explanation of her sinking to
be revised.

It had long been thought that when the Titanic struck an iceberg, a
huge gash opened in the side of the luxury liner. What experts
discovered on examining the wreck told a different story. The damage
was surprisingly small. Instead of a large gash, they discovered six
relatively narrow slits across the six watertight holds.

The newspaper *USA Today* reported this discovery in September

1997 and included this thought-provoking sentence: 'Small damage, invisible to most, can sink not only a great ship but a great reputation.'

As someone once noted, integrity is like virginity—once you lose it, it's gone for good.

I think King David must have understood something about damage below the waterline. In one of his psalms he includes the following prayer: 'Who can discern his errors? Forgive my hidden faults' (Psalm 19:12).

We can often be keenly aware of our most obvious failings and perhaps mature enough to admit to them. But David took things a stage further. He saw his fallen human nature as so flawed that he was unable to identify all its errors. He believed that God's grace was great enough to cover these *hidden faults* and so he acknowledges their existence.

This marvellous film about a tragic ship reminds me to seek God's help for the hidden failures as much as for the obvious ones.

For further reading

EPHESIANS 2:1–9; 1 TIMOTHY 1:12–15

How many of us identify with Paul's description of himself as the 'worst' of sinners? Our natural inclination is to justify ourselves and believe ourselves not to be 'as bad as all that'. It's not difficult to look around and find another person who is a 'much worse' sinner than I am. Or is it? David acknowledged that he had hidden faults but we are aware also of the glaring sins in his life of adultery and murder. Many, perhaps most of us, manage to hide our sins pretty well from others but it's important to remember that those Christians who 'wear their sins on the outside' are no worse than the rest of us. We cannot hide our true selves from God and we all need as much of his grace and mercy as each other.

Prayer

Forgive my hidden faults.
Keep your servant also from wilful sins;
may they not rule over me.
PSALM 19:12–13

Favouritism not allowed

Man looks at the outward appearance, but the Lord looks at the heart.

1 SAMUEL 16:7

You're a busy shop assistant at the end of a long hard day and sales have been dismal. That's bad news, as your predicted bonus for the month is down and you need extra cash for Christmas. Five minutes before closing, in walk two customers—one an elderly lady, expensively dressed and clutching a bulky purse; the second, a scruffy-looking student, wearing faded jeans and battered trainers. How would you handle them?

I've just read a story written by a female journalist who wore five different disguises ranging from a chic, power-dressed executive to a harassed mum with a toddler. She visited a selection of locations and reported the different treatment she received, according to what people believed her to be. From what I read, if you want top service you need to be female, seventy, smartly dressed and look as if you are worth a few bob. I may as well give up now.

It brought to mind some helpful advice: if you want to know the true measure of a person, look at the way they treat someone who can't do anything for them.

The New Testament warns against favouritism, particularly in church. 'Suppose a rich person wearing fine clothes and a gold ring comes to one of your meetings. And suppose a poor person dressed in worn-out clothes also comes. You must not give the best seat to the one in fine clothes and tell the one who is poor to stand at the side or sit on the floor. That is the same way as saying that some people are better than others, and you would be acting like a crooked judge' (James 2:2–4, CEV).

Love is the great leveller that helps us look beyond an image to find the real person. Wes Seelinger, an American clergyman who helps people through dark moments of life, comments:

The intensive care waiting-room is different from any other place in the world. And the people who wait there are different. They can't do enough for each other. No one is rude. The distinctions of race and class melt away. A person is a father first, a black man second. The garbage man loves his wife as much as the university professor loves his, and everyone understands this. Each person pulls for everyone else.

Clothes or no clothes, it's the person underneath that matters.

For further reading

JAMES 2:1–13; ISAIAH 53:2–12

Jesus had time for everyone—for small children, or the sick, the demon-possessed, the immoral, the religious leader with sincere questions. Even in his agony on the cross, he comforted the dying thief. God told Samuel, 'The Lord does not look at the things man looks at. Man looks at the outward appearance, but the Lord looks at the heart' (1 Samuel 16:7). It's very hard, if not impossible, to keep ourselves from assessing people by the way they look. After all, we can't see their hearts. But if we keep in mind what Jesus said—'So in everything, do to others what you would have them do to you' (Matthew 7:12)—then we will begin to learn how we should treat others: with mercy, as Jesus, who was himself 'despised and rejected by men' (Isaiah 53:3), treats us.

Prayer

Lord Jesus, teach me to treat other people the way I would have them treat me. Teach me to look deeper than their outward appearance and to be sensitive to the way they feel. Forgive me for thinking more highly of myself than I ought. Thank you that you love me even though you can see my heart.

Don't speak too soon!

'Do not judge, or you too will be judged. For in the same way as you judge others, you will be judged, and with the measure you use, it will be measured to you.'

MATTHEW 7:1–2

The carriage on the commuter train was only half full when a man and four lively children boarded. The youngsters were rowdy, fighting and pushing each other, shouting loudly. The man sat gazing blankly into space, apparently unconcerned at the children's behaviour. Eventually, after one of them fell over a passenger's outstretched legs, someone challenged the disinterested man. 'Can't you do something to keep your kids under control?' the impatient passenger asked, sensing the support of every adult in the carriage.

The man snapped out of his trance and apologized, acknowledging that, as the father of these bouncy youngsters, he really should have acted sooner. Then he added, 'The truth is, my wife died two hours ago. We are just on our way home from the hospital. I guess my mind is just not on things at the moment. I'm sorry.'

There is a beautiful village in north Wales called Beddgelert. In the thirteenth century, Llywelyn Prince of North Wales went hunting. His dog, Gelert, was unaccountably missing so his master went without him. On Llywelyn's return, his faithful dog came to greet him, but the prince noticed that the animal was stained with blood. He rushed to his small son's bedroom only to find the child's cot empty and bloodstained, bedclothes strewn across the floor. The grief-stricken father concluded that the dog had killed his son so he drew his sword and plunged it into the animal. I quote from the plaque at the dog's grave:

The dog's dying yell was answered by a child's cry. Llywelyn searched and discovered his boy unharmed but nearby lay the body of a mighty wolf which Gelert had slain. The Prince, filled with remorse, is said never to have smiled again. He buried Gelert here. The spot is called Beddgelert.

Two stories centuries apart in time but hardly a centimetre between in impact. They stand as poignant challenges to our natural inclination to jump to hasty conclusions.

Jesus once said, 'Do not judge, or you too will be judged... with the measure you use, it will be measured to you.'

So when your neighbour glares at you this morning, just remember, he may not be angry but in pain.

For further reading

JOHN 4:4–42

Jesus never stopped surprising people. When he asked the Samaritan woman to give him a drink, she was taken aback. Not only was she a Samaritan, and the Jews did not associate with Samaritans, but it would have been very unusual for a religious teacher to speak to a woman in public. No wonder the disciples were surprised when they returned! And as the story unfolds, we discover that Jesus had known all along that this woman was leading an immoral life. In the simple acts of asking for a drink and engaging in conversation, Jesus gave dignity back to this unhappy woman who had failed in making lasting relationships and would have been the object of her neighbours' disapproval and gossip. When we are tempted to disapprove of people because of their lifestyle or their past mistakes, let us remember Jesus' example and treat them with respect and understanding.

Prayer

Pray for someone you find difficult to like or approve of. Ask God to show you some practical way in which you can help and encourage him or her.

Childlike faith

Whoever claims to live in him must walk as Jesus did.
1 JOHN 2:6

The Lambeth Conference is a gathering of the leaders of the Anglican communion worldwide, held every ten years. In recent times, the event has had an agenda loaded with difficult issues that have needed to be faced.

Putting it simply, the task of the Church in every age is to discover God's will and fall in with it. And both sides of that particular proposition are fraught with problems, as each decade's Lambeth delegates will freely admit.

I am not an Anglican but I struggle to find answers to many of the same questions they face—answers that need more than the human skills of diplomacy and political manoeuvring. They require insight and wisdom of the quality that only God can provide.

Mother Teresa used to tell the story of a six-year-old orphan brought into her home in Calcutta. The Sisters rescued him from the streets where he was dying and nursed him back to health.

Once the little boy was fit and well, he was due to be transferred to another orphanage and the Sisters gave him a farewell gift—a small packet of sugar. That doesn't sound much but it is a highly prized commodity among the poor, where a quarter packet of sugar equals a day's wages. As he walked through the gates, the boy saw another small child being carried in from the streets, obviously in great need.

He walked back to the Sisters and handed his packet of sugar over, saying he wanted the sick child to have it. Mother Teresa asked him why he had chosen to do such a thing. 'I think it is what Jesus would have done,' he replied.

That child had a sharp grasp of the ways of God. His action was so simple and yet based on a logical understanding of what following Christ should mean.

John was a man who shared a close friendship with Jesus and who went on to become a key leader in the Church. He once summarized the Christian life in a memorable phrase: 'Whoever claims to live in him must walk as Jesus did.' When faced with tough choices, it's the standard Jesus set that is our sure guideline.

I don't know if the little boy in Mother Teresa's care had ever read that verse. It doesn't really matter.

He knew what it meant.

For further reading

1 JOHN 2:1–11; MARK 10:13–16

In this brief but moving scene in the Gospel of Mark, we learn that children are special to Jesus. In fact, he says, they possess qualities that we all need to emulate if we are to receive God's kingdom. It is noteworthy that throughout John's first letter he addresses his readers as 'children'. Children have little choice but to trust others; they know they cannot survive alone. We know that there is no alternative to trusting God; he is our only, completely sufficient, hope. Children are teachable; they know that they don't know it all. We will live stunted Christian lives if we think there is nothing left for God to teach us. If we are to 'walk as Jesus did' (1 John 2:6), we need to act like the little boy in India, asking not 'What will it cost me?' but 'What would Jesus do?'

Prayer

Lord, I am often very selfish. That little boy's actions put me to shame. I want to become more like you and follow you with childlike faith.

$\mathcal{W}$indows on Family

Just say no!

Teach us to number our days aright, that we may gain a heart of wisdom.

PSALM 90:12

If you had one piece of advice to pass on to someone with life stretched out before them, what would it be? That was the task that fell to Vince Foster, deputy presidential counsel to President Clinton, just six weeks before his death. The advice came from a man who, it seems, committed suicide—although that fact is still a matter of speculation.

Addressing the graduating class at Arkansas University School of Law, he spoke these telling words:

A word about family. You have amply demonstrated that you are achievers willing to work hard, long hours and set aside your personal lives. But it reminds me of the observation that no one was ever heard to say on a death bed, 'I wish I'd spent more time at the office.' Balance wisely your professional life and your family life. If you are fortunate enough to have children, your parents will warn you that your children will grow up and be gone before you know it. I can testify that it is true. God only allows us so many opportunities with our children to read a story, go fishing, play catch and say our prayers together. Try not to miss one of them. The office can wait. It will still be there after your children are gone.

Wise words from a man no longer in this life, with more than a hint of regret lying somewhere at the back of them.

I wonder how many people spend their lives chasing Really Important Things, only to discover, in the end, that they were not that important after all.

Part of an Old Testament prayer, possibly written by Moses, contains the phrase, 'Teach us to number our days aright, that we may gain a heart of wisdom.'

In other words, recognize that what you have is in short supply. Treat it with reverence—and use it with care.

For further reading

DEUTERONOMY 6:4–7; ECCLESIASTES 3:1–13

None of us can be sure how long our life will be or which opportunities will never come again. Even though we may feel that there is never enough time to do everything we feel we ought, if we consider that there are 24 hours in a day, 168 hours in a week and 8,760 hours in a year, we can see that God has made us a generous gift of time. But we need his help and wisdom to know what our priorities should be. We need to learn to say 'no' to some of the demands of life in the modern world, in order to say 'yes' to those things which may seem less urgent but, in the light of eternity, are far more important. The investment we make in other people's lives far outweighs the possessions we accumulate and the status we achieve. Jesus told us, 'Do not store up for yourselves treasures on earth, where moth and rust destroy, and where thieves break in and steal. But store up for yourselves treasures in heaven'—lasting treasures (Matthew 6:19–20).

Prayer

Lord, teach me to live by your priorities and to use your gift of time for things that will last. Help me, each day, to be aware of the needs of those close to me and make me willing to be used to meet them.

Happy ever after

Written in 1995 in the week it was announced that the Prince and Princess of Wales had officially separated.

For this reason a man will leave his father and mother and be united to his wife, and they will become one flesh.
GENESIS 2:24

A young couple sat enjoying their meal in a Texas restaurant. They made an attractive pair, probably in their early years of married life. The area was a farming community and, judging by their look, they probably ran a smallholding and had come into town for supplies.

He got up to pay the bill. She didn't follow him. He came back to the table and stooped down low. She reached up, locked her arms around his neck and, carefully, he lifted her.

Everyone could now see she was wearing a full body brace. She clung to him like a small child as he carried her, gently backing through the entrance and into the parking lot. Everyone in the restaurant watched in silence as he opened the passenger door of the pick-up truck and lowered her gently on to the seat. No one spoke a word, until a waitress said, almost reverently, 'He took his vows seriously.'

In a week when our attention has been focused (perhaps unwillingly) on a prominent couple whose relationship has broken down beyond repair, it is worth turning the spotlight on the rest of us for a moment.

The best man's old one-liner, 'Marriage is a great institution—but who wants to end up living in an institution?' may be so near the mark that it's no longer funny.

Why is it that we won't allow anyone behind the wheel of a car without proper instruction? Or let someone run a playgroup without meeting required standards? Yet we seem content to watch couples set out on married life with nothing more than a big party, a food processor, a set of kitchen knives and a few nudge-nudge comments. That says much about what we prize as important.

Marriages may be made in heaven—but they need to be worked out on earth. And that takes more than luck; it involves skill, dedication, understanding and... help.

For further reading

1 CORINTHIANS 13:1–13; 2 SAMUEL 1:24–27

After Jonathan's death, David paid this tribute to his friendship: 'I grieve for you, Jonathan my brother; you were very dear to me. Your love for me was wonderful, more wonderful than that of women.' The best kind of friends are the ones who give without expecting anything in return. In our marriages and our friendships, we should not be asking, 'When is he/she going to be the kind of husband/wife/friend that I need?' Rather we should ask, 'How can I become the best kind of husband/wife/friend it is possible for me to be?' and let God worry about the other person. The Bible is full of instructions about what real love means and how to build good relationships. All we have to do is to put them into practice.

Prayer

Thank you, Lord, for the gift of friends and family. Help me to become the kind of friend/husband/wife that you would have me be. Teach me to become more concerned with how well I am doing than with how the other person is behaving. I want to become more like Jesus in my relationships.

Freedom and responsibility

It is for freedom that Christ has set us free. Stand firm, then, and do not let yourselves be burdened again by a yoke of slavery.
GALATIANS 5:1

One message of sympathy laid at the scene of her death read simply, 'God's newest little angel.' But the question on most people's minds was, 'Did she have to die?'

Some years ago, seven-year-old Jessica Dubroff was killed in the tangled wreckage of a light aircraft, in which she was attempting to achieve a new world record as the youngest pilot to cross the USA from coast to coast. It seems unbelievable that her parents, the Federal Aviation Authority and the news-hungry media would allow and encourage such a foolhardy stunt. But in a plane adapted to her small frame and accompanied by her father and a flight instructor, this tiny girl (with no more than 35 hours' flying experience) took off in weather conditions that experts have since described as 'ugly'. In attempting to return to the runway after a shaky take-off, the plane stalled and crashed, killing all on board. Whether Jessica or the flight instructor was at the controls at the fateful moment is still unclear.

The debate continues as to the advisability of children attempting such record breaking feats. The *Guinness Book of Records* discontinued its 'Youngest Pilot' categories back in 1989, fearing disasters such as this.

Bombarded with media attention, Jessica's mother defended her support of her little girl's dream. I sympathize with this lady in her grief (and this is not the place to argue the rights and wrongs of the incident) but her words make sobering reading: 'I did everything so that this child could have freedom and choice and have what America stands for. Liberty comes from being in that space of just living your life…'

It is an interesting philosophy and a popular one but it is totally flawed. 'If it feels good, do it!' was a slogan of the 1960s that became a creed of the 1990s. But freedom is a coin with two sides, the flip side bearing the word 'responsibility'. Without both, the pursuit of liberty can lead to anarchy.

The child in the playground snatching a friend's ball is expressing his right to freedom. But ask the one who is left crying how he feels about it and you will get a different perspective. As Jessica's sad story reveals, we can become so obsessed with our rights that we neglect our responsibilities.

Charles Kingsley expressed it well: 'There are two kinds of freedom: the false, when a man is free to do what he likes; the true, when a man is free to do what he ought.'

For further reading

ROMANS 6:1–14; HEBREWS 5:11—6:2

Children need to be trusted with increasing freedom and responsibility for themselves as their parents see that they are able to handle it. They need to have enough knowledge to make wise choices. To give small children total freedom to go where they please and do exactly as they like is to invite disaster. On the other hand, if they are never allowed to act independently their development will be stunted. New Christians have a lot to learn and need patience and help from other believers. The Christian life is not something we arrive at when we are converted but something we have to keep on working at and working out all through our lives. It is very sad that there should be Christians who do not mature, who still 'need milk, not solid food' (Hebrews 5:12). The freedom won by Jesus' death on the cross is not a licence to keep on sinning. We have been 'brought from death to life' (Romans 6:13) so that we can serve God and mature in him.

Prayer

Thank you, Lord, that sin is no longer my master. Help me to enjoy and to use my freedom to serve you.

When is a church like a letterbox?

I have become all things to all men so that by all possible means I might save some.

1 CORINTHIANS 9:22

You can tell a lot about people by their letterboxes. I need to explain the background to this observation, so bear with me.

A longstanding tradition in our family is helping our children with their paper rounds. Having contributed four sons to this noble, undervalued trade, my wife and I have spent years trudging the streets in semi-darkness popping papers through doors.

Actually, 'popping' is the wrong word to use. If the editors of the fat weekend supplements had to deliver these wretched jumbo-sized papers for a couple of weeks, we would witness a drastic change in their size. I have spent many a happy hour, with rain dripping down my neck, trying to squeeze oversized papers through undersized letterboxes.

One Saturday I reached a new low in this Olympic event when my then 13-year-old son hissed at me from a neighbouring house, 'Can you smile a bit as you shove them in, you're giving me a bad reputation!' Kids—I ask you.

So the following week, long before the sun had risen and most of you were out of bed, I made an important discovery. Ninety per cent of British letterboxes are utterly useless for the modern world. They may look good but for the purpose of posting fat supplements they are about as much use as a drive-in burger bar at a health farm. As far as I am concerned, the first political party to put the abolition of undersized letterboxes in their election manifesto gets my vote.

I was recently asked to give an after-dinner speech with the intriguing title, 'Is there any future for the Church in the third millennium?' Among other things, I mentioned the challenge to the Church in every age to adapt to its surroundings. History reveals that church growth has always occurred where Christian leaders have taken risks in building bridges into the prevailing culture. To use the technical term, they have embraced 'incarnational theology'.

As Jesus left heaven to live with us, his followers are called to 'dwell' within their culture and identify with it, but also to challenge and change it. Tragically, many churches are like letterboxes—nice to look at and a bit quaint—but failing to meet the purpose for which they were made.

So if one Saturday you spot a frozen, slightly overweight, forty-something paperboy struggling with your letterbox, please be nice to him.

And, perhaps, even open the door?

For further reading

1 CORINTHIANS 9:19–27

It has been fashionable for a while to talk about 'finding ourselves' and 'voyages of self-discovery'! While there is some value in this, Paul's approach to life was quite different. He was willing to 'lose' himself in order that all manner of people might find Christ. He was single-minded in proclaiming and spreading the gospel but he was also adaptable. There were times when he conformed and times when he refused to, according to how he could best serve God at that time. To Paul, all men and women were worth saving and if that meant becoming 'a slave to everyone, to win as many as possible' (v. 19), he was willing to do it. He uses the illustration of running a race to win the prize to show why he behaves as he does. Winning a race calls for perseverance, sacrifice and dedication but he, and we, are doing it 'to get a crown that will last for ever' (v. 25).

Prayer

Pray for your church and its leaders that you may be responsive to the community in which God has placed you and imaginative in reaching out to those who have not yet received Christ as Saviour.

Rewriting history

O my Comforter in sorrow, my heart is faint within me.
Jeremiah 8:18

The following story is dedicated to those brave members of society who have at one time or another survived the exam season with grit and courage. Sleepless nights, anxious days, missed meals and a hollow, empty feeling telling you that life will never be any different. I am, of course, referring not to the young people who sit exams but to their parents who bravely endure them. The line that says, 'They also serve who only stand and wait…' was never more true.

So to all you bold and battered souls, an apparently true story.

A university student in his final year had spent a whole term without once contacting his parents. Two weeks before he was due home, he wrote the following letter:

Dear Mum and Dad,

I know you haven't heard from me in recent months but the fact is this. A few weeks back there was a fire in my flat and I lost all my possessions. I only escaped with my life by jumping out of a second-floor window. In the process I broke my leg in three places and ended up in hospital. Fortunately, I met the most wonderful nurse there. We fell in love and… well… to cut a long story short, we were married last Saturday. Many of our friends felt this was rushing things but I am convinced that our love for each other will more than compensate for the difference between our social backgrounds and ethnic origins.

By this time, Mum and Dad, I guess you are getting a bit worried. So let me tell you straight away that everything I have written in this letter up to now is completely untrue. I made it all up.

The truth is that two weeks ago I heard that I'd failed my final exams. I just want you to get this news in the proper perspective.

A helpful reminder that win or lose, succeed or fail, we all need to get things into perspective—and a challenge to say a prayer for the children of the world who have known real stress in the killing fields of Rwanda, the bombed wastelands of Kosovo, the streets of São Paulo, the brothels of the Far East and in so many other sad and desperate places.

For further reading

MATTHEW 1:18–25

At times we feel that the bottom has fallen out of our world, especially when our children make mistakes or fail in some way. If we could rewrite history, we would. The Bible doesn't tell us how Joseph felt when he found out that Mary was pregnant with someone else's baby, only that, being a righteous man, he wanted to spare her public shame. To his neighbours it would have appeared that Joseph was a decent man who didn't deserve such misfortune. His openness to God meant that Joseph was able to see that things were not as they at first seemed. Even if, for us, things are as bad as they appear we know that 'in all things God works for the good of those who love him' (Romans 8:28) and he is our 'Comforter in sorrow' (Jeremiah 8:18). If we seek him and obey his leading, we will find a way through the hardest circumstances and as we gain his perspective we may find that things are not exactly as we first thought.

Prayer

Pray for the young people you know, that God would be real to them, that he would protect them from anything that would harm them and that when they act unwisely he would have mercy on them and deliver them from lasting harm.

Soul care

What good is it for a man to gain the whole world, yet forfeit his soul?
MARK 8:36

She looks quite a bit younger than her eighty years allow. She has a mischievous smile, a wonderful sense of fun and a face that looks lived in without being worn out. She resides in a residential home here in the south-west and it was my privilege to have tea with her a few days ago.

Inevitably we talked about the good old days and how things have changed. But what took my breath away was the casual announcement that she and her husband had fostered a staggering total of 47 children during the course of their married life. Each child was seen as special, and most have stayed in touch over the years, no doubt doubly grateful for finding love, security and a home to call their own.

Never one to miss an opportunity, I decided to get some advice. As a struggling parent I thought I would ask someone with the wisdom of the years and, no doubt, the scars to show for it. (Who was it who said, 'Experience is the comb life gives you when all your hair has gone'?)

Did she have anything to pass on? 'Just one thing,' she told me. 'Put as much effort into a child's spiritual welfare as you do into their physical and mental well-being and you won't go far wrong.'

I found myself picking up an echo of Jesus talking about the futility of a person's gaining everything they'd ever wanted… but then ending up losing their soul.

As I rushed to the school gate to meet my eight-year-old, I realized how much we do to ensure that children's bodies are fed and their brains are filled. But what a waste if that is all we do.

My elderly friend was one hundred per cent right. If all we concentrate on is physical and mental development the end result is a lop-sided human being.

Soul care is indispensable for building whole people.

For further reading

MARK 8:31—9:2
Jesus never said that following him would be easy. In fact, he made it quite clear on many occasions that the opposite would be true. When Jesus talked about his own suffering, Peter found it hard to accept and rebuked him. Jesus' words to Peter are quite shocking: 'Get behind me, Satan! You do not have in mind the things of God, but the things of men' (v. 33). Peter had a lot to learn and so do we. We will never be in a position where we will 'know it all' in our Christian lives and we should live humbly with that knowledge. Like children, we too need a lot of 'soul care'. Less than a week after being rebuked by Jesus, Peter was one of the three disciples taken by Jesus to witness his transfiguration. Thank God that he never gives up on us.

Prayer

I am so glad that you do not give up on me, Lord, but like a loving father with a small child you guide me, protect me and, when necessary, rebuke me.

Other people's families

In January 1994, Bishop Haik, a prominent Iranian Christian leader, was brutally murdered.

But Ruth replied, 'Don't urge me to leave you or to turn back from you. Where you go I will go, and where you stay I will stay. Your people will be my people and your God my God.'
RUTH 1:16

Imagine an ordinary day, with your husband going to meet a friend arriving at the airport. Your husband doesn't make his appointment. No phone call, letter or message. He just vanishes.

Imagine reporting his disappearance to the police, only to be met with indifferent bureaucracy, with no one seeming to care what had happened to him. Imagine eleven long days and nights with no news and trying to explain to your children what might have happened to Daddy, always hoping for the best while fearing the worst.

Imagine the telephone ringing and an icy-voiced spokesman of officialdom asking you to come and identify a body found lying in the streets. Imagine the searing pain of discovering that the body is that of your life-partner, and that he had been stabbed to death. Imagine living under a regime where such politically motivated murders are allowed to go unchecked by the authorities. Imagine a land with religion but no justice, with holy places but few holy people.

You don't need to imagine. This is a sketch outline of the horrifying story that affected one family in the country of Iran. The murder victim was a Christian minister, a man by the name of Bishop Haik. He was the chairman of the Council of Protestant Ministers in Iran and widely respected well beyond his own denomination. He was murdered in January 1994, and those who knew him had little doubt as to the reason. He spoke out against the repressive regime that governed Iran and consistently drew attention to religious repression and human rights abuses that were allowed to go unchecked in the nation he loved.

A lifelong friend said of Bishop Haik:

He was a gentle, committed, fearless servant of God. He travelled extensively in Iran to encourage people so they would not be afraid. He stood for integrity and truth. He used to say, 'If there is no religious liberty in Iran, then we will accept that, but when they (the authorities) say there are human rights and religious liberty and, in practice, they are not doing those things, I want this whole world to know about their deception and lies.'

His fearless campaigns on behalf of the voiceless led to his murder at the age of 49, leaving a widow, Takoosh, and four children, the youngest of whom was just nine years old. During the year, memorial services were held all over the world in which prayers were offered for the persecuted in Iran and so many other places.

Let such a man challenge and inspire us as, in a comfortable land, we play in the shallows of Christian belief.

For further reading

RUTH 1:1–22

We have a responsibility to one another. We are part of the same, very diverse, family of God worldwide. Persecuted Christians in other countries draw great comfort from the knowledge that they have not been forgotten by those who enjoy greater freedom. We need to take this seriously and pray regularly for those who are suffering because they worship the same God as we do. And although we rarely suffer physical attack because of our faith in this country, Christians are not immune to violence, serious illness and bereavement. There are people close to us to whom we need to offer support and comfort. Naomi was an unhappy, bitter woman after all that she had suffered but Ruth willingly accompanied her back to Bethlehem. She could not have foreseen and never knew that she would play a significant part in history as a direct ancestor of the Saviour of the world.

Prayer

Pray for families who are suffering because of persecution. Pray that God will give his peace to those who are in prison and concerned that they cannot take care of their families.

Windows on People

More than conquerors

Written a few days after the assassination of Yitzhak Rabin in November 1995.

You are not your own; you were bought at a price.
1 CORINTHIANS 6:19–20

It was the spring of 1955 and the 26-year-old student proudly received his doctorate from Boston University. The professors saw his potential and there were many offers of lucrative lectureships. But he felt the need to experience life beyond university walls, so he opted to become minister of a quiet local church, providing a few years breathing space before devoting himself to his real passion, the world of academia.

A few months later, a black lady had an argument with someone on a bus and the course of this studious young man's life was changed for good.

The lady was Rosa Parks and her refusal to leave a 'whites only' section of a bus in Montgomery, Alabama, launched a local campaign for racial justice. The young pastor of Dexter Avenue Baptist Church, Montgomery, was elected president of the fledgling organization and suddenly found himself at the centre of the national stage.

Dr Martin Luther King Jnr never realized his dream; instead he found his calling.

Eight years later, in Washington DC, when he addressed a crowd of 200,000 peaceful civil rights protesters, he spoke of a different dream, one of justice and equality. He urged his followers to continue their non-violent struggle: 'Let us not seek to satisfy our thirst for freedom by drinking from the cup of hatred and bitterness.' Five years later, in April 1968, he was gunned down in hatred and bitterness on a motel balcony in Memphis.

I was reminded of King's dignified example this week as we mourned the death of another man of peace, Yitzhak Rabin. The soldier-hero turned statesman was murdered by one of his own people, like King, a sacrificial victim on the altar of his own success. I don't know anything of Rabin's personal religious beliefs but I sensed he shared a fervent hope of a better world.

In Martin Luther King's memorable 'I have a dream' speech, he concluded with these words:

When we let freedom ring, when we let it ring from every village and every hamlet, from every state and every city, we will be able to speed up that day when all God's children, black men and white men, Jews and Gentiles, Protestants and Catholics, will be able to join hands and sing in the words of that old Negro spiritual, 'Free at last! Free at last! Thank God Almighty, we are free at last!'

Tragically, great and good men die. The dream lives on.

For further reading

ROMANS 8:28–39

When God has called us to belong to him, our lives no longer belong to us. He may not call us to do anything very spectacular but just to live quiet, faith-filled lives, seeking to please him in very ordinary things. On the other hand, he may call us out to follow him in ways we could not have imagined and might not have chosen, totally different from what we had envisaged for ourselves. In this passage in his letter to the Romans, Paul encourages those whom God has called to take risks for him, even if hardship or death might be the outcome. He expresses memorably his conviction that what we can depend on is God's love for us and that nothing can ever interrupt or extinguish that. Whether we are called to go down in history or not, God's love will never fail us.

Prayer

How good is the God we adore,
Our faithful, unchangeable Friend!
His love is as great as his power,
And knows neither measure nor end!

JOSEPH HART 1712–68

Changed lives

Formerly he was useless to you, but now he has become useful both to you and to me.

PHILEMON 11

A friend recently sent me a gem he'd plucked from the Internet. It is entitled the *Pentekon Bible*, and it covers the message of the world's bestselling book in just fifty words. So if you're counting, here goes:

God made, Adam bit, Noah arked, Abraham split, Joseph ruled, Jacob fooled, Bush talked, Moses balked, Pharaoh plagued, People walked, Sea divided, Tablets guided, Promise landed, Saul freaked, David peeked, Prophets warned, Jesus born, God walked, Love talked, Anger crucified, Hope died, Love rose, Spirit flamed, Word spread, God remained.

Clever stuff. But I am not so sure that it does justice to the greatest story ever told. But then again, I'm not sure how much of what takes place in churches across Britain does justice to it either.

Recently I attended a large gathering in London, called by the denomination I serve. In broad terms we were considering our priorities as churches at the dawn of the new millennium. Much of it was challenging and relevant and I came away grateful that we were at least asking the right questions, even if we had not got all the right answers—yet.

For me, the best moment of the day came in a video report shot in one of the dreariest housing estates in Britain. It featured a woman called Josie and told her moving, yet sadly familiar story. Brought up in council care, drifted into teenage crime, dabbled with drugs and was sent to prison three times in all. She gave birth to her son whilst inside but even motherhood didn't change her lifestyle.

Then a church was opened on the estate, not in an ornate building but in a disused pub. She went in for a few weeks 'for a laugh', as she put it. Then she began to listen to what was being said and, more importantly, began to form a friendship with the people who were there. Bit by bit, Josie began to change. In her own words, 'I never knew what love was, but I do now.'

Josie's life has changed and she now works on her estate running an after-school club for kids who desperately need what she has found—love.

For one church leader at least, the trip was worth it, if only to hear Josie's story and see her face.

The message doesn't have to be clever. Just real.

For further reading

Philemon 1–25

The letter to Philemon is unique among Paul's letters in the Bible. It is not packed full of teaching and instruction but addresses one particular, practical issue, and we are privileged to get a glimpse of Paul's relationship with his friend Philemon. Paul is on very easy terms with Philemon but he has a difficult subject to broach. Philemon's slave, Onesimus, has run away, but it is not only his physical freedom that he has gained, for along the way he has come to know Christ and found true freedom in him. Now he and Paul feel it is right for him to return to his former master, but this is not a simple matter. Onesimus doesn't know what kind of reception he will receive. Under Roman law he deserves death. Paul, in this letter, is trying to prepare the way. He urges Philemon not only to be merciful and receive Onesimus back as a forgiven slave but, more than that, to welcome him back as 'a dear brother' (v. 16). Stories like this one and Josie's 'refresh' our hearts (v. 20).

Prayer

Thank you, Lord Jesus Christ, that you have the power to change lives and turn the useless into the useful. Use me to point others to you.

Forgiveness

Bear with each other and forgive whatever grievances you may have against one another. Forgive as the Lord forgave you.

COLOSSIANS 3:13

Some images live long in the memory. One photograph from the Vietnam War is an image that, some argue, changed public opinion in the USA about their continuance in the conflict. It was a picture of a nine-year-old girl running, naked and terrified, along a street with jellied napalm burning her skin. The look of anguish on her face seared the conscience of a nation caught up in a war it slowly realized could not be won.

Thankfully, that little girl did not remain a stark, anonymous image in a photograph. Her name was Phan Thi Kim Phuc and she was rushed to hospital by the man who took the Pulitzer-winning photo. Kim suffered third-degree burns and underwent years of painful treatment. The damage to her body was so severe that, in the early years, she lost consciousness each time her wounds were cleansed and dressed.

A year or so ago, BBC's *Everyman* programme featured Kim's story, detailing her slow road to recovery. Now, happily married with a small son, she has made a new life for herself in Canada.

Part of her story was a search for personal faith in which she was helped by a Vietnamese pastor. Becoming a committed Christian gave Kim a new perspective on her suffering.

In 1998, Kim attended a ceremony at the Vietnam War Memorial in Washington DC. Speaking to a sea of veterans, once her enemies, she spoke words of forgiveness and reconciliation. 'Sometimes I thought I could not live,' she told them, 'but God saved my life and gave me faith and hope... Even if I could talk face to face with the pilot who dropped the bomb, I would tell him we cannot change history, but we should try to do good things for the present and the future to promote peace.'

Many of the veterans and their families wept openly at the dignified courage of this small woman. Words of hatred and revenge would have been understandable. Instead she spoke words of forgiveness and healing.

History is as much made of the stories of little people as it is of great leaders. Kim Phuc's example testifies that the power of love is greater than the power of hate.

If that is not good news, I don't know what is. And if that one small story were repeated several thousand times over, our world would be a richer place in which to live.

For further reading

LUKE 23:26–47

What did those who were crucifying Jesus think when they heard his words, 'Father, forgive them, for they do not know what they are doing' (v. 34)? It was a strange thing for a condemned criminal to say, while suffering the agonies of being hung on a cross. And it's not surprising that Kim Phuc's forgiveness of those who caused her such suffering should make news. Only God can enable us to forgive the worst things people do to us or to those we love, and it's often something we have to work at over a long time. But what about those small grudges and resentments that we feel justified in clinging on to? How petty they look in the light of these stories. Jesus' prayer for forgiveness was not only for those directly involved in his crucifixion; it was for us as well, because our sin was the reason he submitted to this horrible death. Since we have been forgiven so much, it is only right that we forgive the little that has been done to us.

Prayer

Behold the man upon a cross,
my sin upon his shoulders;
ashamed, I hear my mocking voice
call out among the scoffers.
It was my sin that held him there
until it was accomplished;
his dying breath has brought me life,
I know that it is finished.

STUART TOWNEND

Faith in prison

Remember those in prison as if you were their fellow-prisoners, and those who are ill-treated as if you yourselves were suffering.
HEBREWS 13:3

For me, one of the best things about the summer holidays is the opportunity to catch up on some reading. That may seem strange as my job involves books a great deal, but I find it a change to read things outside my usual diet.

So, for example, I will read three or four of the latest fiction bestsellers and thoroughly enjoy getting lost in the fantasy world of who-dunnits. On one holiday I decided to add to my usual stack of paperbacks a book I had wanted to read for ages—Nelson Mandela's autobiography, *Long Walk to Freedom*.

It is almost 800 pages long and my wife teased that I would take a fortnight to get through. She was wrong. I couldn't put it down, and sat up for two nights until the small hours of the morning until it was finished.

It is a remarkable story about a remarkable man. If it was fiction, it would be classified as brilliant. But it tells a true story of a little boy born into a small village of South Africa's Transkei, who grew up to be one of this century's towering figures on the world stage. For decades his words and even his photograph could not be published in his homeland. He was imprisoned for 28 years and kept virtually isolated from the outside world.

How he rose from a prison island to the presidential palace is a story that must be read. The long struggle for justice and reconciliation in South Africa needs to be widely studied. But the part of Nelson Mandela's story that spoke most clearly to me was his ability to forgive. He stood against the evil of apartheid but seemed to have the capacity to differentiate between a system that was wrong and the people who supported it. It is the principle of 'hating the sin yet loving the sinner'.

He wrote of his prison experience as life-transforming: 'It was during those long and lonely years that my hunger for the freedom of my own people became a hunger for the freedom of all people, white and black. I knew as well as I knew anything that the oppressor must be liberated as surely as the oppressed.'

He may have been in prison but he didn't live as a prisoner. His willingness to forgive set him free long before the cell door opened.

For further reading

PHILIPPIANS 1:1–26

Philippians has been described as an epistle of joy. What is remarkable about this is that it was written by Paul while he was in prison in Rome. He was able to discern advantages for God's work in his captivity and to rejoice in them. Faced with an uncertain future, he was able to talk about choices! He could not decide which he would rather: 'to depart and be with Christ, which is better by far' (v. 23) or to remain and serve God's people by 'fruitful labour' (v. 22). Those of us who do not live in fear of persecution or the loss of our liberty should not make the mistake of thinking that when a Christian believer is put in prison God's work is somehow interrupted. As Paul shows us, God goes on working in quite surprising ways. He has the power to change our perceptions and expectations and bring us joy at our darkest times.

Prayer

Pray for Christian brothers and sisters imprisoned for their faith or because they have stood up for human rights, that they may be able to forgive like Nelson Mandela and rejoice as Paul did.

Friendship with God

Written following the funeral of Cardinal Basil Hume, Roman Catholic Archbishop of Westminster, in 1999.

The fruit of the Spirit is love, joy, peace, patience, kindness, goodness, faithfulness, gentleness and self-control.

GALATIANS 5:22–23

When someone dies, it is expected that people will try to say nice things about them. Part of our acknowledgment of loss is the attempt to express what we most valued about the dead person.

This week the funeral has taken place for Cardinal Basil Hume, leader of Britain's Roman Catholic community. Among the host of tributes, one word recurred—holiness. To those who knew him well, Basil Hume displayed a sense of goodness that pointed to a close relationship with God.

I have been challenged by the common assessment and it has made me think again about what true holiness looks like. The Bible describes the characteristics with the word picture of 'fruit'. Just as you would expect to find apples on an apple tree, we are told the evidence of a truly holy person is seen by the fruit of their character.

In fact, nine different aspects are spelt out: 'The fruit of the Spirit is love, joy, peace, patience, kindness, goodness, faithfulness, gentleness and self-control.'

Curiously, those who most display holiness are least aware of it. But those who watch can't miss it.

Malcolm Muggeridge's film on the life of Mother Teresa, *Something Beautiful for God*, brought to international attention her work in Calcutta. He later told how one scene was shot in a dark building, and the cameraman, Ken Macmillan, feared that nothing would come out.

When the film was processed, the interior shots were bathed in a wonderful, soft light that no one could explain. Muggeridge later wrote:

I have no doubt whatever as to what the explanation is: holiness, an expression of life, is luminous... The camera had caught this luminosity, without which the film would have come out quite black, as Ken Macmillan proved to himself when he used the same stock in similar circumstances and got no picture at all.

Holiness is not reserved for a handful of people but is God's desire for everyone. But as a tree needs good soil, solid roots and correct nourishment, so growing a holy life requires the right conditions.

Basil Hume (without setting himself up as an ideal example) wrote about the starting point: 'Holiness involves friendship with God. There has to be a moment in our relationship with God when he ceases to be just a Sunday acquaintance and becomes a weekday friend.'

Wise words from a truly *good* man.

For further reading

JOHN 17:6–26

We may sometimes think that holiness is a special state reserved for 'super Christians' and not for people like us who lead unremarkable, ordinary lives. But holiness is a much more mundane thing than we may be tempted to believe and something for each of us to work out in our everyday lives. When Jesus prayed this prayer for his disciples, he knew that he faced denial and abandonment by them that very night. And yet he prayed, 'Glory has come to me through them' (v. 10). They, like us, were very unpromising material but because of their relationship with Jesus it was possible for them to bring him glory. As Cardinal Hume's words implied, holiness develops out of our relationship with God and it is that relationship that we need to work at, not at achieving holiness by our own efforts.

Prayer

I don't want to 'conform any longer to the pattern of this world' (Romans 12:2). Lord, transform me by the renewing of my mind as I spend time getting to know you better.

Challenging prejudice

Written in the week the Report of the Enquiry into the death of teenager Stephen Lawrence was published in February 1999.

'Do not judge, and you will not be judged. Do not condemn, and you will not be condemned. Forgive, and you will be forgiven.'
LUKE 6:37

When teenager Stephen Lawrence bled to death on a London street on 22 April 1993, he had no idea he would become so famous. His parents, Neville and Doreen Lawrence, dearly wish he wasn't. Their son was murdered in an attack that lasted seconds but its implications have run for years.

This week's landmark report into the Lawrence murder is an indictment of a culture that has allowed racism to flourish. It may (we hope) become what Home Secretary, Jack Straw, describes as 'a catalyst for permanent and irrevocable change, not just across our public services but across the whole of society'.

The big question that I am left with is, 'How?' It is good to hear promises of changes in the law and tightening up of rules for the public services—these are big steps in the right direction. But no government can pass laws that change attitudes and that is where the real battle must be won.

Racism is not confined to the housing estates and football terraces. You find it in many corners of community life, including the Church.

I have preached a fair number of sermons over the last three decades and faced congregations from chapels to cathedrals. I know that there are certain 'hot buttons' you can press to get a 'good Christian reaction'.

Abortion, homosexuality, the anti-Christian bias of the press, the lowering of sexual standards and the breakdown of marriage are guaranteed a few hearty nods and grunts of approval even in churches where excitement is usually expressed by raising the left eyebrow s-l-o-w-l-y. But racism will only attract a blank look from even the most evangelical congregation. Believe me, I've tried it. It ranks alongside world poverty, inner-city deprivation and anything to do with money as a real killer for any sermon.

The Stephen Lawrence enquiry report remains a wake-up call we all need to hear.

During the apartheid era in South Africa, a young black boy was walking along a street with his mother when a tall white man passed them and greeted the pair by raising his hat. The boy was amazed. Fancy a white man raising his hat to a black woman! 'Why did he do that?' he asked his mother. 'Because he is a priest,' she replied. 'I want to be a priest,' the boy declared.

The name of the priest was Trevor Huddlestone. And the small black boy was Desmond Tutu.

In the battle to change attitudes, example remains the sharpest blade.

For further reading

LUKE 7:36–50

Throughout the Gospels we get glimpses of Jesus encountering all sorts of people. No one who came to Jesus was turned away. Jesus did not set out to offend 'respectable' people by intentionally mixing with those on the fringes of society but it was inevitable that he would. When Jesus accepted the attention of this woman while in the home of a Pharisee, it was wrongly assumed that he did not know her reputation. If Jesus had been running an earthly campaign for acceptance and popularity as a religious leader, he would have been very unwise to let the woman do what she did. But Jesus' wisdom was always the wisdom of love that saw the intentions of the heart. He was never inhibited by what other people might think of him but welcomed anyone who approached him. Nobody can grow up totally free from prejudice of one kind or another. We absorb unconsciously the attitudes of those around us. Like Simon, the Pharisee, we need to have our thinking challenged and we need to be very careful whose examples we follow.

Prayer

Help me, Lord, to catch myself when I am tempted to think that I am better than someone else, for whatever reason. Help me to follow your example of showing love and respect to everyone I meet, seeking to see the person underneath and not to be influenced by outward things.

$\mathcal{W}$indows on the Beatitudes

How to avoid embarrassment

'Blessed are the poor in spirit, for theirs is the kingdom of heaven.'
MATTHEW 5:3

Harvard University was proud of its new Philosophy Department. The authorities approached a noted academic to suggest a suitable inscription for the lintel over the door of the new building. He recommended a line from Protagoras, the Greek philosopher: 'Man is the measure of all things.'

When the building was opened, the academic was surprised and annoyed to discover that his advice had been rejected. The University bypassed his suggestion and settled instead on a quotation from the Bible: 'What is man that thou art mindful of him?' (Psalm 8:4, AV).

Much of our modern dilemma can be understood in the difference between those two statements.

The first comes from a human-centred view of the universe, the second from a God-centred view. The first leads us to focus on rights; the second on responsibilities. The first teaches if God exists at all, then he is accountable to us; the second, that we are accountable to him. The first fuels our pride; the second humbles our souls.

Jesus knew the value of a soundbite. As a good teacher, he wanted to make his teaching stick, and he often used easy-to-learn phrases and images. A group of these statements in the Gospels are known as 'the Beatitudes' (which comes from a word meaning 'blessing'). Over the next few studies we shall be looking at them in turn.

The first reads, 'Blessed are the poor in spirit, for theirs is the kingdom of heaven.'

There's no fun in being poor but that is not what Jesus is saying. Being poor in spirit is all about having a right estimate of yourself. In terms of relationship with God, honesty is always the best policy. I can fool my wife, the boss and even the man next door, but not God. Jesus is saying that the way 'up' in God's eyes is the way 'down' in our own.

Real happiness and joy (a better description of the word 'blessed') comes when we're honest to God. The wonderful irony is that once we realize how poor we are, we can discover how rich God intends us to be. The whole of the kingdom of heaven belongs to those who are prepared to stoop and enter.

In the words of Augustine, 'For those who would learn God's ways, humility is the first thing, humility is the second, humility is the third.'

For further reading

LUKE 14:7–14; PHILIPPIANS 2:5–11

Jesus was eating at the home of a 'prominent Pharisee' (Luke 14:1) one Sabbath when he commented on the tendency in all of us to want the best places and to push ourselves forward. He gave good, practical advice for avoiding embarrassment but he was also pointing out the deeper truth, that in God's kingdom 'everyone who exalts himself will be humbled, and he who humbles himself will be exalted' (Luke 14:11). This is the example that Jesus himself set for us. As the passage in Philippians shows, Jesus chose to give up his high position in heaven to come to earth as a man in order to serve and to die for us. Because of this, 'God exalted him to the highest place' (Philippians 2:9). Jesus then turned to his host to apply what this attitude of humility should mean to him. When we have a true estimation of ourselves, we will be able to reach out to those to whom society would assign a lower place, not in a patronizing way but as we ourselves would like to be treated.

Prayer

Lord, I acknowledge my poverty before you and thank you for the riches that are mine through what Jesus has done for me.

Joyful mourners

'Blessed are those who mourn, for they will be comforted.'
MATTHEW 5:4

To equate happiness with a broken heart sounds plain daft. But that is exactly what Jesus did in the second of the beatitudes: 'Blessed are those who mourn, for they will be comforted.'

At one level, Jesus is referring to the nearness of God in our moments of grief and personal loss. At such times, many have found peace and comfort in a way they never thought possible.

But there is a deeper meaning. When this beatitude is read along with the others, we see that Jesus is describing the character of a person living in God's kingdom. The Beatitudes give a photofit of someone who is serious about following Christ. In the light of this, the mourning Jesus refers to is more than the pain of bereavement, it is a deep-seated sense of grief because of our sin. He is teaching that only when we are broken by our own sense of failure can we experience the kiss of God's forgiveness and the embrace of his grace.

Although it is becoming increasingly popular to blame our failure on others ('It wasn't my fault; my genes made me do it!'), Jesus points to the responsibility of owning up to our failures. There is no question of ducking the issue or pointing the finger.

I know that there is such a thing as false guilt, and that unscrupulous people sometimes play on that to their own advantage. But equally, there is a false sense of freedom when we try to take short cuts by avoiding blame instead of facing it. This beatitude reminds us of the importance of squarely facing up to the fact that we have broken God's law, offended his character and have no claims on his kindness whatsoever. In the words of the prayer of confession, 'there is no health in us...'

Jesus points us to the source of all forgiveness—God himself. He not only comforts broken hearts but heals them as well. Through the power of the cross, we are able to discover forgiveness and the power to start again. But the connection to this comfort comes when we are willing to admit we are wrong.

Theologian and philosopher Samuel Clarke (1675–1729) once wrote, 'Nothing will make the faces of God's children more fair than for them to wash themselves every morning in their tears.'

This is not a licence for miserable Christians—rather, joyful ones.

For further reading

PSALM 51:1–19

We cannot get through a single day without sin of some sort and we need to be conscientious about coming to God for his free and ungrudging forgiveness. But there are times when we do something which we bitterly regret, that cannot be undone, when we find it hard to believe that God can forgive us and feel that we will never be able to forgive ourselves. We may feel that we cannot bear to face God but at times like these we do need to come, as David did in this psalm, to the God of 'unfailing love' and 'great compassion' (v. 1). Jesus died to set us free from sin and guilt. He bore the punishment for us. It is God's will to restore the joy of our salvation to us when we come to him with 'broken and contrite' hearts (v. 17). Whatever anyone else may think, he will not 'despise' us.

Prayer

Lord, 'wash away all my iniquity and cleanse me from my sin' (Psalm 51:2).

The benefits of meekness

'Blessed are the meek, for they will inherit the earth.'
MATTHEW 5:5

We now consider the third beatitude, which I once saw parodied in a piece of graffiti: 'The meek will inherit the earth (that's if it's OK with the rest of you)!'

This illustrates how we can misunderstand the word 'meek'. We confuse meekness with weakness but that's a long way from the truth. What Jesus actually said was, 'Blessed are the meek, for they will inherit the earth.'

I recently saw a TV documentary about a man who specializes in training horses. The programme showed him with a dangerous, uncontrollable mustang. Yet, within a few days, the trainer had brought the horse to the point of being able to take a bit, bridle and saddle. The same horse that had lashed out in anger and fear was now peacefully led through its paces with a mounted rider. The trainer emphasized that he had not used whips and fear but had relied on building a relationship with the animal in which trust could grow.

It so happens that the word translated 'meek' in the Bible is also used to describe a horse which has been broken in. Meekness does not mean weakness but rather controlled strength. The mustang had lost none of its strength; instead, that energy had been channelled to maximum effectiveness. Once it had been running wild; now it was running free.

Aristotle defined meekness as the balance between extreme anger and excessive angerlessness. The meek man gets angry at the right time but never at the wrong time. Reading the beatitude in this light destroys the myth that to be meek means being a pushover, afraid of standing up for what you believe.

But what does it mean that the meek will inherit the earth? This is an example of God's 'upside-down values'. It may look as if the selfish, arrogant go-getters are the ones who win. But don't put the book down until you've read to the end of the story. In the long run, it is those who live lives directed and controlled by God who will succeed.

Like the remarkable horse-trainer I watched on television, God has our best interests at heart. To be controlled by him is not to lose our identity but to discover what we are really made for—running free.

For further reading

PSALM 37:1–40

This psalm tells us not to 'fret' about the kind of people who trample on the meek. It tells us that we should not concern ourselves with them because their prosperity will be short-lived. Our concern is to 'delight' ourselves in God who will give us the 'desires' of our hearts (v. 4). He will help and deliver us. We are instructed to be patient when we see people succeeding in 'their wicked schemes' (v. 7). We are not to get upset or brood resentfully. In the sequence of history there is a time when 'the meek will inherit the land and enjoy great peace' (v. 11). Even if the wicked seem to have things all their own way right now, we can be sure that their reign is coming to an end. In the meantime we can put our trust in God who is our 'stronghold in time of trouble' (v. 39).

Prayer

Help me, Lord, to strike the right balance between acting against injustice whenever possible and not fretting when I see wickedness apparently flourishing. Thank you that history is your story and that your justice will have the last word.

The route to fulfilment

'Blessed are those who hunger and thirst for righteousness, for they will be filled.'
MATTHEW 5:6

There's dedication and there's downright fanaticism. The story of a Chinese fighter pilot taught me a lesson about the difference between the two.

Art Chen fought in the 1930s conflict between China and Japan. Chen engaged three Japanese planes in a dogfight. He shot down the first, then ran out of ammunition. He deliberately rammed the second, bailing out before impact. Landing close to the wreckage, he salvaged one of the machine guns and carried it across country for eight miles to his airbase. Presenting the heavy gun to his CO, Chen allegedly asked, 'Sir, can I have a plane for my machine gun?'

There's a man with the sort of all-consuming passion that makes a fanatic. It is the passion Jesus refers to in the fourth beatitude: 'Blessed are those who hunger and thirst for righteousness, for they will be filled.'

The Beatitudes paint a picture of what a follower of Christ looks like. Each begins with the word 'blessed', which to our ears may sound religious, dull and unattractive. But the word refers to the deepest experience of joy it is possible to imagine.

Jesus teaches that a mark of discipleship is a deep hunger and thirst for righteousness. He deliberately chooses two of our most basic appetites to make his point. It symbolizes a burning desire to live a life that pleases God and is ruled only by the wish to do his will. It means not opting for the comfortable route of public opinion when setting our values, but a steely determination to live by God's rules.

I freely admit that I often fall well short of the target. In fact, I often find myself aiming in the wrong direction. But that is where the hunger and thirst analogy is so helpful. Jesus does not say 'blessed are the righteous', rather 'blessed are those who hunger and thirst after righteousness'. The Christian faith is often described in terms of a battle and that is never more apparent than in our own internal struggles. But the blessing wrapped up in this beatitude is that a passionate pursuit of God and his righteousness leads ultimately to fulfilment.

As Gulf War hero, General H. Norman Schwarzkopf, put it, 'The truth of the matter is, you always know the right thing to do. The hard part is doing it.'

For further reading

PSALM 42:1–11

We are reminded by this psalm that, although there are times when everything about the exercise of our faith in God comes easily, when it is a delight to meet with others to worship him, when our prayers flow easily and living to please him seems only natural, at other stages of our life faith is a struggle. For some it may be that illness interferes with the routines of worship, both public and private. For others apathy may just creep up on us. When God seems far away, we need to hunger and thirst for him anew, to keep on seeking him and reminding ourselves of all that he is to us and all that he has done. When we reawaken our hunger and thirst for him, we will find again the satisfaction that he promises.

Prayer

If living the Christian life is easy and spontaneous for you at present, praise God 'with shouts of joy and thanksgiving' (v. 4).

If you are struggling, if God seems far away, say with the psalmist:
> *Why are you downcast, O my soul?*
> *Why so disturbed within me?*
> *Put your hope in God,*
> *for I will yet praise him,*
> *my Saviour and my God (v. 5).*

Don't shoot your enemies

'Blessed are the merciful, for they will be shown mercy.'
Matthew 5:7

Revenge, they say, is a dish best eaten cold. After all, if you are going to get your own back, you might as well enjoy the experience. 'Don't get mad, get even' is the bumper sticker summary of the attitude which refuses to forgive and forget.

All of this is in stark contrast to the words of Jesus in the fifth beatitude: 'Blessed are the merciful, for they will be shown mercy.' Previously Jesus spoke of those who are hungry to please God and, in case anyone ran away with the wrong idea about holiness, he earths his point in no-nonsense terms. Holiness is not about a list of religious rules of dos and don'ts but it is about how we live and deal with other people.

Being merciful in our dealings carries important implications. First, you can only show mercy towards people who don't deserve it. By its very nature, mercy is a gift instead of a pay-back.

Second, it is an active thing rather than just a feeling. In the story of the Good Samaritan (which is all about mercy), the traveller didn't just stand by the side of the road feeling sympathetic to the mugged stranger; he did something practical to meet his needs.

Third (and this is the tough bit), the way we deal with others affects how God deals with us. It is the merciful who are shown mercy—or, in the words of the prayer Jesus taught his disciples, 'Forgive us our sins, for we also forgive everyone who sins against us' (Luke 11:4). This is why on Sundays in churches and chapels across the country, some will go in and come out the same way they went in—hard, cold, angry and bitter. And that will have little to do with the length of the sermon, the volume of the organ or the state of the boiler. It will be because of an unforgiving spirit.

Ramon Narvaez was a Spanish general who rose to the office of Prime Minister in the nineteenth century. As he lay dying, a priest asked, 'Does Your Excellency forgive all his enemies?' Narvaez replied, 'I do not have to forgive my enemies, I have had them all shot.'

Whether with real bullets or imaginary ones, that is one option, according to Jesus, that a genuine Christian can never take.

For further reading

MATTHEW 18:21–35

In this parable, both the servants use similar words when they ask for more time to pay their debts. However, the first servant, who was forgiven an enormous sum of money, fails to make the connection between being shown mercy and showing it in turn. He refuses even to give the other man more time in order to pay his debt, let alone cancelling such a small amount. We immediately see the connection, and so did the other servants and the king in the story. Is it possible that we who so easily see the speck of sawdust in someone else's eye and miss the plank in our own (Matthew 7:3) are missing connections in our own lives between the way God has treated us and the way we treat others? Jesus' words in verse 35 are uncompromising. We ignore them at our peril.

Prayer

Ask God to show you if there are inconsistencies in your life between the way he has treated you and the way you treat others. If you have failed to forgive someone who has wronged you, ask God to give you the desire and the ability to do so.

Spotting the fake

'Blessed are the pure in heart, for they will see God.'
MATTHEW 5:8

Do you ever dream of finding something really valuable tucked away at the back of the attic? Part of the strong appeal of TV programmes such as the BBC's 'Antiques Roadshow' is based on this kind of hope, and occasionally an expert will cast their eye over something that may look like 'junk' and declare it far more valuable than its owner imagined.

The sixth beatitude reads, 'Blessed are the pure in heart, for they will see God.' At the heart of true religion lies the desire to know God. Jesus states that this is possible but with an important qualification: such a privilege is available to those whose hearts are pure. The word 'pure' means clean or unmixed with other things. It points to our motives which we may be able to hide from others, but not from God.

For example, it is easy to fall into the trap of appearing to help someone in need when in reality we are helping ourselves. Or we can give the impression we are one thing when in truth we are the opposite. We mask our real feelings with the expert skill of the chameleon, changing our colours to suit our surroundings.

Joseph Stalin, the Soviet dictator, died following a massive seizure brought on by a fit of rage during a heated argument at a meeting of the Presidium. As he crashed to the floor unconscious, a man called Lavrentio Beria, a member of the inner circle, began to dance around the body shouting, 'We're free at last! Free at last!' As Stalin received medical treatment, he momentarily stirred and opened his eyes. At once Beria stopped his celebrations, dropped to his knees and began to kiss Stalin's hand with all the supposed grief of a loyal supporter.

In this beatitude, Jesus underlines that 'unmixed' thinking, motives and actions are the marks of true holiness. Like the antiques expert, God is able to spot the fake and recognize the genuine. And the special blessing he brings to those whose hearts are pure is the ability to see, know and understand God.

Purity of heart sounds dull and boring. But the pure heart leads to the fulfilled life and sets us free from the tyranny of hypocrisy.

As Mohandas Gandhi wrote, 'There is nothing worse than being something on the outside that you are not on the inside.'

For further reading

TITUS 1:1–16

Paul writes to Titus with detailed instructions on the appointment of elders who must be 'blameless'. Verses 5 to 9 give a practical description of blamelessness, referring to how the elder should conduct his family, social and business life. He is to 'hold firmly' to the gospel he has been taught in order to 'encourage others' and 'refute those who oppose' the truth. The description of those who are qualified to be elders contrasts strongly with those 'rebellious people, mere talkers and deceivers' (v. 10) who are more concerned with ceremonial purity than with inward, personal purity. When Paul says, 'To the pure, all things are pure, but to those who are corrupted and do not believe, nothing is pure' (v. 15), he is pointing out that just as rituals and ceremonies cannot make someone pure, neither can the neglect of them make those who are right with God impure. Not only do we need to be pure in our thinking, motives and actions, we need to be discerning about the leaders that we listen to.

Prayer

Give me a pure heart and a discerning mind, that I might not be led astray by those who do not truly know and follow you, Lord Jesus.

God's business

'Blessed are the peacemakers, for they will be called sons of God.'
MATTHEW 5:9

Thomas Edison was responsible for around 1300 inventions, the most famous of which is the electric light bulb. His son, Charles, opted for a career in politics and, campaigning for the Governorship of New Jersey in 1940, he was anxious to point out that he was not relying on his famous father's reputation. He declared, 'I would not have anyone believe I am trading on the name of Edison. I would rather have you know me merely as the result of one of my father's early experiments.'

The sixth beatitude reminds us that family associations cannot fail to be recognized. Jesus said, 'Blessed are the peacemakers, for they will be called sons of God.'

The Beatitudes provide a photofit of a true follower of Jesus. The sixth in the list highlights the importance of being a bridge between people, and it's a timely reminder in a world often riddled with divisions.

Jesus doesn't speak of peace-lovers—those who will do anything for a quiet life. Nor does he talk of peace-keepers—those who direct their efforts to prevent people tearing each other apart but never addressing the problem that set them at odds in the first place. Instead he refers to peacemakers.

These are those willing to bear the cost of making reconciliation possible, and that price often involves being misunderstood by those we are seeking to help. I recall a situation in my own life when a close friend and I disagreed over something that threatened to end our friendship. Someone took the time and trouble to sit us both down and work through the issues that had clouded our horizon. He could have avoided getting involved—or, worse still, could have added a few more bricks to our wall of silent separation. But instead of pouring petrol on the flames, God used him to pour oil on troubled water.

Those who act in this sort of way cannot hide the family likeness. Reconciliation is God's business and those who make it their priority are doing God's work. The Jewish rabbis taught that the highest service a man can perform is to establish right relationships between people.

In the words of Abraham Lincoln, 'Die when I may, I would like it to be said of me that I pulled up a weed and planted a flower where I thought a flower would grow.'

For further reading

1 SAMUEL 25:1–39

Abigail was a truly wise peacemaker. Her intervention not only saved the lives of many people but also prevented David from acting rashly and having on his conscience, as Abigail so vividly expressed it, 'the staggering burden of needless bloodshed or of having avenged himself' (v. 31). She reminded him that his calling was to fight 'the Lord's battles' (v. 28), not his own. David restrained himself from taking his own revenge, but about ten days later he heard that God had 'brought Nabal's wrongdoing down on his own head' and that Nabal was dead (v. 39). We need to learn that if we are zealous for God's cause then he will take care of us. We do not need to defend our rights or our reputations. Jesus is our rock 'and the one who trusts in him will never be put to shame' (Romans 9:33).

Prayer

Make me a channel of your peace.
Where there is hatred let me bring your love;
where there is injury, your pardon Lord;
and where there's doubt true faith in you.

PRAYER OF ST FRANCIS

Persecution is a blessing

'Blessed are those who are persecuted because of righteousness, for theirs is the kingdom of heaven.'
MATTHEW 5:10

Unless there is something odd about their personality, no one enjoys being victimized. News reports of school bullying or discrimination in the workplace are rightly met with condemnation. To pick on a person because of their colour, religious belief, gender or simply because they are somehow 'different' is, thankfully, generally accepted as unacceptable.

Perhaps that is why the words of Jesus in the eighth beatitude are hard to understand: 'Blessed are those who are persecuted because of righteousness, for theirs is the kingdom of heaven.'

The Beatitudes paint a picture of what a follower of Christ should look like. Characteristics such as humility, a hunger for God and striving after justice are easy to understand. But to include in the list a willingness to endure persecution appears strange, at least at first glance.

Jesus is pointing out that suffering is a badge of discipleship, and history shows that there are times when men and women of faith have been called upon to die wearing it. That is not something confined to the past. The other day I read a disturbing report quoting a prestigious research body, claiming that an estimated 160,000 Christians have died for their faith over a twelve-month period. It is claimed that more Christians have been martyred in the twentieth century than in the previous nineteen combined. Thousands of others, belonging to different faiths, have also been murdered, demonstrating that intolerance, sadly, is still alive and active.

But you don't have to travel far to find such prejudice. There are those in Britain today who suffer in a hundred hidden ways for their faith. Snide remarks, isolation and being passed over for promotion may not hurt as much as an electric cattle prod, but they represent a smaller, though not less significant, cost of wearing the badge.

Following Christ means having the courage to be different. And that will always run the risk of attracting the attention of those who can't stand the possibility of an individual standing out against the system. But as Jesus points out, those willing to pay the price of such courage receive the greatest prize of all: 'Blessed are you when people insult you, persecute you and falsely say all kinds of evil against you because of me. Rejoice and be glad, because great is your reward in heaven' (Matthew 5:11–12).

For further reading

1 PETER 1:3–9; 4:12–19

There are 'all kinds of trials' that cause us to 'suffer grief' (1 Peter 1:6). We may not be put in prison or tortured for our faith, we may not risk losing our livelihoods, but we may lose our friends or suffer painful estrangement from our families. It is tempting to keep our heads down and remain quiet about what we believe. When we stand out for what is right, we make other people with lower standards feel judged and criticized (even when that is not our intention) and they want to put us down. It is certainly not pleasant to have people avoid us, tell lies about us or misrepresent our motives but if we seek to receive this as a blessing from God rather than an insult from our persecutor, then God can use it for his good purposes—to refine our faith and to bring glory to him. And, as Peter tells us, we should not be discouraged and give up but 'continue to do good' (4:19).

Prayer

Lord, it's hard to stand up and do what is right when I know it's going to make me unpopular, but help me to keep my eyes fixed on you. I want to please you and I believe that one day you will reward me for all I suffer now.

*W*indows on Following Christ

Perseverance

Jesus replied, 'No one who puts his hand to the plough and looks back is fit for service in the kingdom of God.'
LUKE 9:62

The 400th anniversary of the death of one of the south-west's most celebrated figures has given rise to controversy. Was Sir Francis Drake a hero or a crook?

Personally, I find Sir Francis a magnetic man who typified the adventurous spirit of his age. As the Elizabethan historian, John Stow, commented, 'He was more skilful in all points of navigation than any... He was also of perfect memory, great observation, eloquent by nature...' His detractors, so it seems, resented his humble roots and his un-willingness to bend the knee to those who felt they were his social superiors. If that is true, he sounds even more like a hero to me!

Some years ago I came across a prayer that Drake is reported to have written around the time of his attack on the Spanish harbour of Cadiz in 1587, which he referred to as 'singeing the King of Spain's beard'. Without delving into the morality of war and those who wage it, and recognizing that Drake lived as a child of his time (as we all do), it is interesting to see the sense of duty conveyed in the words of his prayer:

O, Lord, when thou givest to thy servants to endeavour any great matter, grant us also to know that it is not the beginning but the continuing of the same until it be thoroughly finished which yieldeth the true glory.

I have often been struck by the true grit of that prayer, which strikes a contrasting note to our quick-fix society where bailing out is usually seen as preferable to battling through. In Drake's day, when sea voyages took months or even years, patient endurance was par for the course.

When the *Golden Hind* returned to the Atlantic Waters during Drake's epic round-the-world voyage in 1580, only 56 of the original crew of one hundred were left aboard.

As we salute the memory of this great seafarer, it is worth remembering this lost quality of perseverance which we new Elizabethans seem sadly to lack.

Billy Graham once asked the President of Harvard University to sum up the greatest need of today's students. 'Commitment,' he replied.

And that, it seems, is a need that traverses the Atlantic Ocean as surely as Drake and his fellow mariners did four centuries ago.

For further reading

HEBREWS 10:19–39

It is easy to lose momentum as time passes. In one sense this is natural: as we age, our bodies become less able to do things we did without thinking when we were younger. But, as Christians, our momentum should be increasing because God 'is coming... and will not delay' (v. 37). In eternal terms, time is short. The writer to the Hebrews looks back to 'those earlier days after you had received the light' when no sacrifice of reputation or possessions seemed too great (v. 32). Even those who were not actively persecuted took the risk of standing 'side by side with those who were so treated' (v. 33). Now, however, they seemed to have lost that earlier enthusiasm. Paul urges them, and us, not to 'throw away your confidence', because our perseverance will be rewarded (v. 35). When we look back on the past, it should not be to 'rest on our laurels' but as an impetus to even greater service.

Prayer

'O, Lord, when thou givest to thy servants to endeavour any great matter, grant us also to know that it is not the beginning but the continuing of the same until it be thoroughly finished which yieldeth the true glory.'

Don't laugh

Shout for joy to the Lord, all the earth.
PSALM 98:4

According to Dickens's Mr Bumble, 'The law is a ass—a idiot.'

I think he has a point, particularly when you consider some outdated laws that remain on the statute book, quietly dozing but never roused. I wonder what Mr Bumble would have made of a list of laws from Alabama that I recently came across.

Apparently in this fine American state it is an offence to wear a false moustache, drive blindfolded, keep an ice-cream cone in your pocket and make people laugh in church. So if you are planning a visit to the deep South, be warned.

On the basis that every action has a reaction, I'm left wondering what led to such laws in the first place. Was there a spate of armed hold-ups in churches involving a gang who heavily disguised themselves, reduced their victims to helpless hysteria and threatened them with a large cornet before robbing them blind? Think about it, there must have been a good reason somewhere back in time.

Obviously the one that grabbed my attention was the law making it illegal to make people laugh in church. Now before I get a spate of letters reminding me about the importance of reverence, let me say I'm all for it. Church is not meant to be a religious attempt at 'Sunday Night at the Palladium'. But anyone who has studied communication will know that laughter is a strategic weapon in any speaker's box of tools.

Study the teaching of Jesus and you'll notice that some of his sayings were designed to raise a smile—and make a point.

Worship is when we give ourselves to God, and that involves all that we are as people, including our emotions. A well-known verse in the New Testament deals with giving money as part of worship and says,

'God loves a cheerful giver' (2 Corinthians 9:7). The word 'cheerful' in the Greek language is *hilaros*, from which we get our English word 'hilarious'. It means open-hearted, generous and happy to give.

What an amazing thought—a million miles away from the sombre, lacklustre and mind-numbing boredom that is often passed off as a service of worship.

So next time you're in church and the plate comes round, dig deep, give generously and grin. Or perhaps a little chuckle. And if you're really bold, a full-blown burst of the giggles.

But please, not in Alabama.

For further reading

DEUTERONOMY 16:13–17; PSALM 98:1–9

The book of Deuteronomy can sometimes seem rather dry to read with all its detailed regulations, but it also contains details of feasts and celebrations because God had promised to bless the people of Israel if they obeyed him. Our times of celebration are usually fairly curtailed, a few days at the most, but the Feast of Tabernacles lasted seven days and the Israelites were instructed to 'be joyful at your Feast' (Deuteronomy 16:14). Everyone, men and women, rich and poor, old and young, were to be a part of the celebration. Gifts were to be brought to show how God had blessed them and make them think about why they were there. Psalm 98 gives us a taste of a noisy Jewish celebration. It reminds us that we have something wonderful to celebrate: 'The Lord has made his salvation known' (v. 2), and the psalmist doesn't suggest we keep quiet about it!

Prayer

Were the whole realm of nature mine,
That were an offering far too small;
Love so amazing, so divine,
Demands my soul, my life, my all.
ISAAC WATTS (1674–1748)

Loose rudders

'So, if the Son sets you free, you will be free indeed.'
JOHN 8:36

The phrase 'up the creek without a paddle' has a new meaning as far as I am concerned.

I was enjoying a peaceful afternoon's sailing on one of Cornwall's delightful waterways. The sun shone and the wind was blowing at just the right speed as I cruised along in a one-man dinghy loaned by a friend. As a comparative beginner (this was my first solo run), I was understandably nervous, but as the minutes went by my confidence grew.

Then disaster struck. Without warning, the rudder came loose from its fitting and in my struggle to retrieve it I overbalanced, tipping the boat precariously to the side. I watched, utterly helpless, as the rudder, with the tiller attached, slid over the stern and down into the depths of the river, never to be seen again.

For those readers who don't sail and may be wondering what the fuss is about, let me explain. Imagine driving a car at 40mph on a busy dual-carriageway when the steering wheel just vanishes into thin air and—here's the interesting bit—you can't stop the car from moving because the accelerator is jammed.

Half my problem was that I couldn't steer the boat—the rudder had vanished overboard. The other half of the problem was the sail flapping around in a wind that decided it was time to blow a bit harder. I won't bore you with the details of what happened next, other than to say that (a) what I did has probably never appeared in any training manual; (b) the new rudder cost £120 plus some helpful advice on how to handle dodgy fittings; and (c) I didn't get wet. Oh yes, I should add (d) I didn't lose my temper when my wife tactfully said, 'Worse things happen at sea!'

That uncomfortable sailing experience had a familiar ring. I've known what it is to be driven on without any control over my direction. Powerful forces, and not all of them good, can hit us stronger than any gust of wind. Anger, jealousy, lust, greed—it can be a long list. As I have learned to my cost on many occasions, self-control is not strong enough to withstand some forces. We need a power stronger than ourselves and greater than those things that would drive us in the wrong direction.

Jesus said, 'If the Son sets you free, you will be free indeed.'

For further reading

JAMES 3:1–12; PROVERBS 15:1–33

James compares the tongue to, amongst other things, the rudder of a ship. He says that although the tongue is only a small part of our body it is nevertheless very hard to control. The danger is that if we don't control it, our whole lives will be steered off course. As James points out, the person who is able to control his tongue so that he 'is never at fault in what he says' will be disciplined in every area of life (James 3:2). Proverbs 15 is interspersed with wise comments on how we may use our tongues for good—to defuse anger, bring healing and say the right thing at the right time. We are advised to cultivate the habit of thinking before we speak (v. 28). If we can do this successfully, with the help of the Holy Spirit, it follows that we will lead lives characterized by godly self-control.

Prayer

Teach me to do your will, for you are my God;
may your good Spirit lead me on level ground.
PSALM 143:10

Taxing times

Give everyone what you owe him: If you owe taxes, pay taxes; if revenue, then revenue; if respect, then respect; if honour, then honour.

ROMANS 13:7

Every year, the dreaded date comes round. Around the country, people realize to their horror that there are only two days left. I am talking about filing your Tax Return. I usually end up completing mine at the last minute, promising myself each time that next year I will be much more disciplined about getting the wretched thing in sooner.

On one occasion I decided to visit the Tax Office for myself, fearing that if my return was held up in the post I'd miss the deadline. (Secretly, I was hoping they may give out stickers or stars if you made a personal call.)

I don't think I had ever before had the pleasure of calling in personally at the Inland Revenue, so I was unsure what to expect. I assumed it would be a cold and uninspiring place, populated by a group of grey, grim-faced accountants in shiny suits—and I was pleasantly surprised.

I entered a bright, warm building to be greeted by a charming lady on reception who looked as if she belonged in a travel agency. She took my return, carefully noting down the details in a register, and gave me a glowing smile into the bargain. Was there anything else I needed? Well, there was just one question. If I wanted to take a seat in the reception area she was sure someone could help... actually the queue was very small at the moment, so I probably would have no more than five minutes to wait if I could spare the time in my busy day?

I left the office (having received a cheerful 'thank you and goodbye') and found myself standing in the car park with a mixture of pleasant feelings. It was a bit like going to the dentist for a check-up and finding that nothing needed to be filled or fixed.

Perhaps I picked a good day or an extra-nice receptionist, or maybe the Inland Revenue has hired a charm school instructor. All I know is, I came away feeling more like a client than a schoolboy handing in his homework late again.

All of which set me thinking… about cold church buildings, PA systems that fail to work properly, stern faces, cold handshakes, archaic language, boring sermons.

A simple lesson really. How we act affects what people think about us—and what we have to offer.

For further reading

MARK 12:13–17; ROMANS 13:1–14

We may be citizens of a heavenly kingdom (Philippians 3:20) but while we are on earth we have to deal with all the bureaucracy that being a citizen here entails. Paying taxes is not the most enjoyable part of life but, as Paul taught, it is necessary for us to submit ourselves to 'the governing authorities' because they 'have been established by God' (Romans 13:1) and are themselves, whether they acknowledge it or not, servants of God 'to do you good' and 'to bring punishment on the wrongdoer' (v. 4). We obey earthly rules and regulations to bring glory to God. This is not to say that our governments will always behave in ways that honour God or treat individuals fairly but, unless to submit to them would entail disobeying God, we must do as Jesus said and 'give to Caesar what is Caesar's and to God what is God's' (Mark 12:17). And that includes being scrupulous about declaring all our income and paying the tax due on it.

Prayer

Pray that God will guide and bless all those in positions of authority in this country, that he will help them to bear the burdens of responsibility and of sometimes having their motives misunderstood, and that he would help them to act wisely and courageously to govern us fairly and well.

Something for nothing

'...remembering the words the Lord Jesus himself said: "It is more blessed to give than to receive."'
ACTS 20:35

Picture the scene—a crowded shopping centre on Saturday morning. A creeping queue edges into the car park. Having found a space, impatient shoppers line up to feed the 'Pay and Display Machine' before getting down to the serious business of the day.

But today is different. A group of youngsters are standing by the ticket machine. They accost customers with a polite question: 'How many hours would you like to stay?' On receiving the answer, one of the teenagers feeds in some coins and passes the ticket over with a 'have a nice day' kind of smile. The shoppers assume that either the machine is broken (again) or the Council have another crazy youth employment scheme for jobless yobs. They offer payment for their tickets but are politely refused. Sensing a catch, the shoppers try again but meet the same response.

Come on, we all know there's no such thing as a free lunch. There must be a catch. It's rag week, worse still 'Beadle's About'—'Where's the hidden camera, then?' 'No catch, no camera, we simply wanted to do something to make your day. Honest.'

After an hour, the police arrive. A spy-in-the-sky camera had trained on the youngsters as they'd started trading. Drugs, intimidation, or are they selling without a licence? A squad car was despatched to check it out. No, they couldn't believe it either. 'There must be an angle we're missing, Sarge. They're clean and look nice kids. But you don't get something for nothing, eh?'

Addresses are taken and stories checked. It all tallies. They are a bunch of youngsters from a local church. Christians, it seems. Heard a sermon about loving people and decided to do something about it. So they organized a whip-round and collected about £60 to go to the local shopping centre and give something for nothing. When asked to explain themselves, they muttered about wanting to show how God loves people unconditionally, and how giving things and serving others was one way that his love could be reflected in the world.

Strange stuff. But it actually happened in an Essex town not so long ago. A little piece of good news for a change—and a poignant, practical demonstration of some other Good News that goes on changing people for the better, every day of the week.

For further reading

DEUTERONOMY 15:1–11

It is not God's will that anyone should be in need when others have plenty. Verse 11 says, 'There will always be poor people in the land' but verse 4 says that there shouldn't be, since God plans to bless the Israelites 'richly' if they obey him. This passage makes it plain that to have and to withhold from the needy is a sin. God built into the Israelites' calendar a year every seven years for cancelling debts so that no one should sink deeper and deeper into debt without hope of escape. But he knew that human nature meant the better-off would be tempted not to lend when that time was approaching because of the likelihood of not being repaid. God does not want 'hard-hearted' and 'tight-fisted' followers (v. 7). This passage is talking about generosity in *lending* to the poor, but if we *give* freely without expecting repayment, even better.

Prayer

Lord, as you have blessed me and met my needs, help me to be open-handed and generous to those in need.

Hard work

Whatever you do, work at it with all your heart, as working for the Lord, not for men, since you know that you will receive an inheritance from the Lord as a reward.

COLOSSIANS 3:23–24

If you happened to be an employee of Carson, Pirie and Company, Chicago, in 1858 you would have been confronted with this frightening Staff Code of Conduct:

Store must be open from 6am to 9pm the year round. Store must not be opened on the Sabbath, unless necessary to do so, and then only for a few minutes. The employee who is in the habit of smoking Spanish cigars, being shaved at the barber shop, going to dances and other places of amusement, will surely give his employer reason to be suspicious of his integrity and honesty. Each employee must pay not less than $5 per year to the church and must attend Sunday School regularly. Men employees are given one evening a week for courting and two if they go to the prayer meeting. After fourteen hours of work in the store, the leisure hours should be spent mostly in reading.

You can't help but wonder how many job hunters took one look at the rules and decided to take their search elsewhere!

The EC's determination to establish a Europe-wide pattern for a minimum wage and maximum working week sparked an intense debate in this country. Some argued the case for justice with a fair day's work deserving a fair day's pay and the right of every individual to be protected from sweat-shop conditions. Others contended that profitability and increased employment prospects demanded minimum interference from governments. It would be fascinating to see how Carson, Pirie and Co. would have fared at the hands of the Strasbourg Court of Human Rights.

The first Christians lived in a world vastly different to ours. Many were slaves with no rights and a few were slave owners with unlimited powers. In several places in the New Testament, working relationships come up, usually in the form of explaining how following Christ should affect the world of work. Slaves were encouraged to work hard, and not simply when they were being watched. They were to work 'as working for the Lord, not for men'. Masters were instructed to 'provide your slaves with what is right and fair, because you know that you also have a Master in Heaven' (Colossians 3:23; 4:1).

It is interesting that bosses and workers alike are reminded that their lives are to be lived under God's scrutiny. After all, true justice is his prerogative. A thought worth remembering in the current debate?

For further reading

MATTHEW 20:1–16

'Pursuing a career' has superseded 'earning a living' and, for some people, takes priority over family life. We can find ourselves being brainwashed into believing that there is a 'basic' standard of living we should all aspire to, which includes owning a TV, video, home computer and two cars and taking a holiday abroad once a year. The media feeds the idea that 'having' equates with happiness. Although this parable is primarily concerned with the heavenly principle that 'the last will be first, and the first will be last' (v. 16), it does teach us a lesson about contentment. Instead of comparing ourselves to other people, we should keep our eyes fixed on God and all that he provides us with, both materially and spiritually. If we look at other people, we are bound to become dissatisfied, but if we look at what God has done for us how can we be anything but grateful?

Prayer

Teach me, Lord, to be content with what I have. Deliver me from the temptation of wanting what other people have. I trust you to provide all my needs.

Windows on Pain

God's best photo

For in Christ all the fulness of the Deity lives in bodily form.
COLOSSIANS 2:9

Not so long ago, the Pope publicly dismissed as inaccurate, descriptions of God as an old man with a beard who lives in the sky.

That may have come as quite a shock to some. I have met a few people who are convinced God lives somewhere in Surrey, enjoys cricket, listens to Radio 3 and reads the *Daily Telegraph*.

But the comment prompts an interesting question. What is God like? A national newspaper once published an interview with a six-year-old girl named Katie Lee. Her views on the subject ran like this:

There's one God and he's the creator of heaven. God is Jesus' father. God has glasses, I think. I don't think God has animals in the air. I think God has animals on the ground and he comes down and feeds them. I think God has not got a cooker in the air. He comes down and has takeaways. He tries lots of different sorts because there's lots of people in the world. God likes Indian and Japanese but I think he likes MacDonalds best. I think he has coffee to keep him warm.

Then this tiny theologian added this poignant comment: 'He's normally fair but sometimes not. Daddy's secretary was only twenty-nine and she died in a car crash. Why wasn't God looking?'

I think Katie echoed the kind of question we all ask from time to time—and one to which there are no slick answers.

Whether we are six or ninety-six, we all suffer a type of blindness that makes our understanding of God blurred, to say the least. If we rely on our own feelings, we end up with a picture of God as a nine-foot man, just a little bigger than our puny selves.

God is spirit and totally different from us, not just in appearance but in character too. When the Bible talks of God having eyes, ears, hands and feet, it's using language to help our understanding.

God is invisible to the human eye but he chose not to leave it like that. Jesus came to make the invisible visible. The Bible says, 'No one has ever seen God, but God the One and Only, who is at the Father's side, has made him known' (John 1:18).

As a poster I once saw outside a church read, 'Jesus is the best photo God ever had taken.'

For further reading

JOB 1:6–12; 42:1–17

Is God fair? No, he's not. If he were, he would not have allowed Jesus to die for our sins; we would have had to pay the price ourselves. God is not fair, but he is just and merciful. Of all people, Job was the least deserving of the awful suffering he had to endure and it took him a long time to be able to come to the place where he could say, 'My ears had heard of you but now my eyes have seen you' (42:5). It is often through suffering that we come to know God in a special way that would not be possible otherwise. When we look at the suffering around us or in our own lives, it's understandable that we ask, 'Where's God? Why is he letting this happen?' and God does not turn his back on our sincere questioning, even if he doesn't show us the whole answer right away. However, we can take great comfort from the fact that Jesus was 'a man of sorrows, and familiar with suffering' (Isaiah 53:3) and he really understands.

Prayer

Lord, I look at people around me and I see the pain of broken relationships, disappointments and illness. I watch television and see people caught up in the midst of war and natural disasters, and I feel so helpless. Help me to use the opportunities I have to tell people about you and the hope and comfort that you can bring to them.

Grief takes time

Written in 1994 in the week of the sudden death of Labour leader, John Smith.

Jesus wept.

JOHN 11:35

Numbed. Shocked. Disbelieving. Angry. Just a selection of the words used to report reaction to the sad news of the death of Labour's leader, John Smith. For a time—and quite rightly—party politics are laid on one side as someone who was held in respect and affection by colleagues as well as opponents is mourned. This news has touched us all, reminding us of our frail humanity. In the words of John Donne: 'Any man's death diminishes me, because I am involved in Mankind; and therefore never send to know for whom the bell tolls; it tolls for thee.'

For those who have experienced bereavement themselves, such a sudden death of a public figure brings back their own personal pain. Our prayers and thoughts will be with Elizabeth Smith and her three daughters over the next few days. But what then?

Grief goes on long after the funeral. For many, that is the point when the painful, long-haul of grieving begins.

I once heard an interview on the radio with someone involved in counselling victims of the awful sectarian murders in Northern Ireland. When asked of the practical problems faced by those whose family members have been brutally killed, he replied, 'For too many of us grief has a sell-by date. There's a time when we think people should be over it. And we don't seem to understand when they're not.' There speaks the voice of experience.

Grief takes time. A long time. And people who grieve deserve support and care well beyond the time when the news first breaks and the funeral service is held.

If you, like me, have been touched by John Smith's tragic death, then look around in your own circle of contacts over the next few days and think of any who have suffered bereavement. Maybe you could make a phone call, write a letter, call and see them, check how things are going.

And perhaps out of the sadness, those who feel it more keenly can find help and, through that, hope.

For further reading

JOHN 11:1–44

Verse 35 of John 11 may be the shortest verse in the Bible but its significance is far greater than its length. 'Jesus wept.' But why did he weep? After all, only a short time later he was going to bring Lazarus back to life. This was not a spur-of-the-moment decision in response to his grief or the grief of others; he had already told his disciples, 'Our friend Lazarus has fallen asleep; but I am going there to wake him up' (v. 11). So why did Jesus weep? Was he weeping for those he saw grieving, for Martha and Mary in their distress? Or was it because one day Lazarus would die and not be brought back to life on earth? Did Jesus weep in that moment for all the deaths and all the sorrow caused by bereavement that ever had been and ever would be in this fallen world? Whatever the reason, we can be assured that Jesus meets with us in our sorrow. He feels for us in our grief. And, what is more, we have the promise that one day 'God will wipe away every tear' from our eyes (Revelation 7:17).

Prayer

If you are grieving, whether for a recent loss or for one that happened some time ago, thank God that he understands and feels for you.

For others, ask God to make you aware of those around you who may be sad, perhaps at a particular time of year or on certain occasions when their loss is brought home to them again. Pray that he will show you how to reach out and comfort them.

Where is God when it hurts?

And we know that in all things God works for the good of those who love him, who have been called according to his purpose.
ROMANS 8:28

Where is God when it hurts? Why do bad things happen to good people? And if God is all-powerful, why is the world in such a mess?

When the headlines tell of ethnic cleansing, bombing campaigns, and massacres even in schools, it's not surprising that such questions keep coming back.

They are reasonable questions too and, in case you were wondering, they are ones I often ask myself in times of pain. And they neither have nor deserve slick answers. Anyone who can explain the problem of evil with a few Bible verses has either never seen hurt or never been hurt.

Bereft of easy answers, I draw strength from five foundational truths the Bible reveals about God's nature and character.

First, God is not immune to suffering. The rejection, betrayal and horrific death of Jesus attest that God has identified with human pain at its deepest level. Second, God is just and will not allow evil to go unchecked for ever. You reap what you sow, both in this life and the next.

Third, God is involved with those who suffer. Find pain and you discover his frontline troops near at hand, offering comfort and help.

Fourth, God is able to bring good from bad. Even the darkest situations have traces of light, often provided by those moved beyond their own self-interests.

Fifth, God can help faith to grow through the hard experience of suffering. I admit that this is the toughest of the five, as sometimes people lose their faith through tragedy, perhaps concluding that it is no longer worth believing in a God who appears to have stood idly by as pain struck. But for each person who has turned away I have found many more whose faith has grown through hard times. Pain, it seems, has the potential to either draw us to God or drive us from him.

Even Nietzsche (who believed God was dead) acknowledged, 'He who has a *why* to live can bear with almost any *how*.'

This was eloquently expressed in a poem found in a cave where a group of Jews sheltered from the Nazis.

> *I believe in the sun, though it is late in rising.*
> *I believe in love, though it is absent.*
> *I believe in God, though he is silent.*

With our pain and our questions, may God give us grace to find him somewhere in the silence.

For further reading

ESTHER 4:1–17

Esther faced a difficult choice between two risky alternatives at a time of crisis. All she had to go on were Mordecai's assurance—'Who knows but that you have come to royal position for such a time as this?' (v. 14)—and her reliance on God as she told Mordecai to ask all the Jews in Susa to fast for her. She literally took her life in her hands when she approached the king, but God was at work behind the scenes. The book of Esther is full of apparently unrelated occurrences that God weaves together to bring about the thwarting of Haman's murderous plans, the deliverance of the Jews and the belated honouring of Mordecai. Sometimes we need to be reminded that God is working in *all things* for our good and, however dark life seems to be, he will not let us down.

Prayer

Be my rock of refuge,
to which I can always go;
give the command to save me,
for you are my rock and my fortress.
PSALM 71:3

Light in the darkness

Written during the week of the historic papal visit to Cuba in 1998.

The light shines in the darkness, and the darkness has never put it out.

JOHN 1:5 (GNB)

This weekend, world attention will focus on the island of Cuba. In a historic visit, Pope John Paul and communist dictator, Fidel Castro, will embrace and an estimated 3,000 foreign journalists will report on a series of religious services.

Such events were unthinkable a few years ago. Forty years of militant communism has dominated every aspect of Cuban life and the Christian Church has had its share of pressure. This is hardly surprising for a state that came to regard the words of Lenin as gospel, for as he wrote, 'Everyone must be an atheist. We will never attain our goal until the myth of God has been removed from the thoughts of men.'

But, as Comrade Fidel and his friends have discovered, you can't erase the indelible.

A fervent religious faith has flourished in Cuba in spite of opposition. I recently listened to a BBC reporter relating stories of growth in various religious movements on the island, the largest being among evangelical Christians.

In Havana's Plaza de la Revolucion, the symbolic heart of Castro's regime, a new image was added as part of the Papal preparations. Alongside a statue to Jose Marti and a bronze sculpture of Che Guevara, two of Cuba's greatest heroes, another portrait appeared. The figure of Jesus now dominates the square, bearing the slogan 'Jesus Christ—in you we trust.'

I am reminded of an event in the Chinese city of Chungking during the Cultural Revolution of the 1960s. Bibles, prayer and hymn books were confiscated and publicly burned. Christians were forced to watch this denunciation of their faith. Someone managed to conceal a charred page from the bonfire and it became a prized possession among the persecuted Church. This single page from the Bible was read and re-read among congregations for years. Its very preservation became to the suffering Church a symbol of hope.

Years later, as China began to open its doors to the world, a Western Christian leader checked the story's authenticity. He was particularly keen to discover what part of the Bible had sustained the Church through the lonely years of persecution.

The page was part of Matthew's Gospel which contains the following prophetic statement of Jesus: 'I will build my church, and the gates of Hades will not overcome it' (Matthew 16:18).

Something to ponder as we witness some remarkable scenes in Cuba this weekend.

For further reading

JOHN 1:1–18; REVELATION 22:1–5

The light from a candle is barely noticeable in daylight but a candle in a dark room stands out distinctly. However extensive the darkness, it cannot render the tiny flame invisible. In the dark days of persecution and oppression, Christians stand out. They have no choice. Unless they deny their beliefs, they cannot blend in, and their suffering makes the flame of their faith burn brighter in contrast to the surrounding darkness and evil. But the day is coming, the book of Revelation tells us, when our small lights will be lost for ever in the overwhelming, uncreated light of the Lord God. Jesus, 'the true light' of the world who came so many years ago to bring hope to a sin-darkened world, will be our 'bright Morning Star' (Revelation 22:16) dawning on a day that will never end and we, amazing though it may seem, will reign with him for ever.

Prayer

Father in heaven, may my light shine before men so that they may see my good deeds and praise you (Matthew 5:16).

Whom shall I fear?

The Lord is my light and my salvation—whom shall I fear? The Lord is the stronghold of my life—of whom shall I be afraid?

PSALM 27:1

Back in 1947, *The Bulletin of the Atomic Scientists* established a Doomsday clock to warn of impending nuclear danger. It was set at seven minutes to midnight, dropping to three minutes in 1949 when the Soviets exploded their first atomic bomb and to two minutes in 1953 when the US tested its first hydrogen bomb. The clock was moved a little back and forward until it reached ten minutes to midnight in 1990. On 26 November 1991 the *Bulletin* announced its 'optimism that we are entering a new era' and reset the clock to an unprecedented seventeen minutes to midnight. But it warned, 'The world is still a dangerous place, still containing some 50,000 nuclear warheads and still pouring vast sums of money and intellectual capital into weaponry at the cost of economic distortions of human misery.'

So with the clock reset you would think we could all sleep a little easier at night. But we know different. With one threat receding, there is always another rising. As the wise old saying puts its, 'There are no solutions, only new problems.'

I remember once sitting with an elderly lady who had not many days left on earth. We talked and laughed as she reminisced about a full and happy life. But, she confided, there were still worries that kept her awake at night and concerns that she found hard to express even to those closest to her. We talked about that line in Henry Francis Lyte's famous hymn that runs, 'Change and decay in all around I see: O Thou who changest not, abide with me.' She spoke movingly about her deep trust in God who had taken her safely through some difficult days over the years.

Here was a pilgrim preparing to break camp and move on to better quarters. So I read her a pilgrim psalm, written by King David over three thousand years ago. Its message is fresher than today's milk: 'The Lord is my light and my salvation—whom shall I fear? The Lord is the stronghold of my life—of whom shall I be afraid?'

Her tired face crinkled with a smile of sheer joy as she repeated the words.

You see, ultimately it matters little where the hands of the clock are set. What leads to true peace of mind is knowing whose hands are holding yours.

For further reading

PSALM 91:1–16

We live in a frightening, threatening world. This psalm vividly describes the horrors of sickness and war, which are already so familiar to us (even if we have not experienced them firsthand) through what we read in the newspapers and see on television almost daily. It is not surprising that there are times when we feel apprehensive and fearful but the psalmist tells us that this is unnecessary. If we are living in close and intimate fellowship with God then we need not be afraid. At first reading, it might appear that the psalm is saying that those who trust in God will not suffer from these things, but what God actually promises is that he will be with us 'in trouble' (v. 15); he will 'rescue' (v. 14) those who love him. Whatever the future may hold for us, good or bad, we need not worry because God will be with us to defend and to comfort us.

Prayer

Abide with me: fast falls the eventide;
The darkness deepens; Lord, with me abide!
When other helpers fail, and comforts flee,
Help of the helpless, O abide with me.
HENRY FRANCIS LYTE (1793–1847)

Hope

Written in September 1995.

Gladness and joy will overtake them, and sorrow and sighing will flee away.
ISAIAH 35:10

Imagine home was a floating rubbish tip shared with 10,000 others, and your main means of making a living was sifting through piles of rotting waste. Dwellers on Smokey Mountain in the Philippines don't have to imagine—it's real life, 365 days a year.

Smokey Mountain hit the news a while back as the Philippine government announced plans to rehouse 3,000 families in a clean-up operation. Cynics note that the Asian leaders' summit—due to be held in Manila next year—may have prompted the government to deal with an embarrassing eyesore.

Whatever the motive, it's good news for the inhabitants of the world's largest rubbish dump. Constant risk of fire through methane gas, landslides prompted by rain, craters appearing as rubbish settles are a few of the daily hazards faced by dump dwellers—not to mention the perils of disease in a rat-infested environment.

I will never forget my visit to Smokey Mountain, seeing refuse trucks lining up outside the site met by bands of eager volunteers, ready to pick their way through other people's rubbish to earn a few *pesos* by selling reclaimed tins, bottles and rags. But it wasn't the poverty, the over-powering stench or the smouldering piles of rubbish that lived on in my memory. It's the hope that I remember.

My companion, a Filipino aid worker, took me to the six churches, the medical clinic and the kindergarten all housed on the site. We visited families in their cardboard and plywood houses and watched children playing amid piles of junk.

I met people who were bright, happy and industrious—children who were mischievous, noisy and playful. I heard plans for the development of community life and saw evidence of practical love being demonstrated. My heart leapt when I read of a prospect of better things for the people of Smokey Mountain—even if it has taken more than forty years to get there.

We may feel frustrated by hosepipe bans or even plagued by noisy neighbours but none of us can begin to imagine how privileged we are, compared to so many.

Walking through the debris of Smokey Mountain I recalled a haunting phrase: 'I used to complain about the colour of my shoes—until I met a man without any feet.'

For further reading

Isaiah 35:1–10

Have you ever met someone with nothing going for them who none the less speaks out of a thankful heart and makes you ashamed of your own petty grumbles? It's amazing to see hope flourishing in places where you'd least expect it. When Jesus died on the cross, from the disciples' point of view it looked like the end of everything. How wrong they were! It was really the beginning. So when, humanly speaking, our situation is bleak and frightening and seemingly hopeless, let's not give up hope but put our trust in God's promises, made hundreds of years before their fulfilment and some still to be realized. Jesus, who was prepared to give his life to bring us hope has a purpose even in our darkest circumstances.

Prayer

Lord, when doubts fill my mind, when my heart is in turmoil, quiet me and give me renewed hope and cheer.

Psalm 94:19 (Living Bible)

Was God in Dunblane?

Written in the aftermath of the Dunblane massacre in 1996.

Weeping may remain for a night, but rejoicing comes in the morning.
PSALM 30:5

News this week of the demolition of the school gymnasium in Dunblane reminds us of the attempts of this shattered community to rebuild their lives. The bulldozing of the building is a profound symbol of this brave city's attempt to look to the future, without denying the past.

Of all the thousands of words that have been written about Dunblane, I was struck by the report of a clergyman, John Drane, who was called with other colleagues to offer pastoral help to the community. One evening he found himself at the gates of the primary school where the murders took place. A gang of youths had gathered, bringing sixteen nightlights—one for each dead child. There followed an awkward silence. One of them, recognizing him as a clergyman, called Drane across and asked him to say something appropriate. Let me quote his report:

As I stood there, tears streaming down my face, I had no idea what to say or how to say it. Words had not been especially useful to me, or anyone else in this crisis. So we stood holding on to one another for a moment, and then I said a brief prayer. That was the catalyst that enabled them to start praying. A question came first: 'What kind of world is this?' Another asked, 'Is there no hope?' Someone said, 'I wish I could trust God.' 'I'll need to change,' said a fourth.

As he did so, he looked first at me, and then glanced over his shoulder to the police who were on duty. He reached into his pocket and I could see he had a knife. He knelt down by the ring of candles and quietly said, 'I'll not be needing this now', as he tucked it away under some of the flowers lying nearby. One of the others produced what looked like a piece of bicycle chain and did the same. We stood silently and then went our separate ways.

John Drane concludes his moving account with these words: 'Was God in Dunblane? Of course. How could I have been so foolish as to doubt it?'

God is not the author of evil—neither does it take him by surprise. In the most horrific of evil's twisted forms, he can be found if we are prepared to look.

And that is what urges us to continue praying in hope for the people of Dunblane, and for all those who have survived great tragedies.

For further reading

PSALM 30:1–12; REVELATION 7:13–17

We cannot tell those who are suffering how they can find signs of hope or the strength to go on. Our clumsy words of comfort often hinder healing rather than help. A story like the one above, coming out of the horror of Dunblane, is a comfort to those of us who can only imagine what it must have been like to be part of that community. Psalm 30 promises hope to the one who finds him or herself in 'the depths', that the pain will not go on for ever. The night of weeping may last a long time and seem almost unendurable but God's intention is that 'rejoicing' will come 'in the morning'. And a time is coming when there will be no more suffering because God has promised 'never again...' (Revelation 7:16).

Prayer

'We do not know what we ought to pray for, but the Spirit himself intercedes for us with groans that words cannot express' (Romans 8:26). Thank you, God of comfort.

Out of despair

This is the day the Lord has made; let us rejoice and be glad in it.
PSALM 118:24

What do you do when you believe life has no point any more?

Someone who knew something of that bleak despair invited a visiting preacher to stay in her home. The lady in question, who had been widowed for several years, gave up her bedroom for her guest while she slept in the small boxroom.

Waking early the next day, the guest threw back the curtains and looked at the magnificent view—rolling hills, clusters of trees, and hedgerows alive with all the glories of an English spring morning. The man stood and stared as the sun's early morning rays gently stroked the day alive. It was breathtaking.

As he drank in the view, the preacher noticed some marks on the window pane: THIS IS THE DAY.

At breakfast he commented to his hostess about the glorious view from her window and inquired about the words on the glass.

She explained that she had written them using the diamond on her well-worn engagement ring. She had done it as a permanent reminder of a special experience in her life.

Slowly the story unfolded of a woman overwhelmed with bleak despair, having lost a life-partner. The magnificent view from the bedroom window so admired by her guest was not always as inviting. There were mornings, she admitted, when she looked out on wet, windswept hills that mirrored the cold emptiness inside her. She told the guest of days when she simply wanted to stop living. Since her husband's death, life had lost its meaning.

One day she had turned to the Bible and read a verse she had known since childhood, but its relevance struck her in a new way: 'This is the day the Lord has made; let us rejoice and be glad in it.'

The woman explained to the preacher, 'God showed me my life did have a purpose and I was to treat each day as a special gift. My time would come one day but in the meantime I could greet each new day with faith instead of despair.'

She continued, 'I scratched those four words, "This is the day", as a reminder of God's promise to me. Whatever the weather and however I am feeling, I can look into each day through the promise of God.'

For further reading

1 Kings 19:1–18

Defeating the prophets of Baal and ending the three-year drought was probably the high point of Elijah's career but he came down to earth very swiftly when Jezebel threatened his life. Despite all the evidence that God was with him, 'Elijah was afraid and ran for his life' (v. 3). Exhausted, he asked God to kill him and promptly fell asleep. Elijah had seen miraculous answers to his prayers but this was one prayer God chose not to answer. Instead he sent an angel to tend to Elijah's physical needs. When we are in despair or discouraged or simply weary, God understands and he doesn't condemn us. Only when Elijah was restored and physically ready did God reveal to him that he was to go back and continue with his work by anointing a prophet to succeed him and a new king for Israel.

Prayer

Let the morning bring me word of your unfailing love,
for I have put my trust in you.
Show me the way I should go,
for to you I lift up my soul.
Psalm 143:8

Windows on Heaven

Meeting the deadline

I wait for the Lord, my soul waits, and in his word I put my hope.
PSALM 130:5

I once heard a joke that was doing the rounds, involving President Clinton, Fidel Castro and Microsoft magnate, Bill Gates. The three receive a message from God that the world will end in a week. Clinton addresses the American people, declaring, 'My fellow Americans, I have good news and bad news. The good news is, there is a God. The bad news is that the world will end next week.'

Castro broadcasts to the Cubans, 'Comrades! I have bad news and even worse news. The bad news is, God does exist, and the worse news is, he is about to end the world.'

Bill Gates goes on the Internet, 'Greetings, Microsoft users. I have great news and even better news. First, God thinks I'm one of the three most important men in the world. Second, we won't have to upgrade Windows 2000.'

If you are a computer buff (or buffoon in my case), you will get the joke. My friend who told it to me did—and could hardly get to the punchline for laughing.

But the good news/serious news/sobering news is that the world will end one day—and that's no joke.

I have recently been studying New Testament passages that teach about the end of history. It won't end with a whimper or a bang—but a coronation. Excuse me—The Coronation. For example, 'With a loud command and with the shout of the chief angel and a blast of God's trumpet, the Lord will return from heaven' (1 Thessalonians 4:16, CEV).

There are more references to the second coming of Jesus than to his first and, throughout the centuries, people under intense persecution have drawn great comfort from this. After all, if you are a victim of injustice and oppression, the hope of a better tomorrow probably helps you cope with the agony of today.

But the second coming of Christ not only 'comforts the disturbed', it also 'disturbs the comfortable' because it raises the question, 'How are we living now in the light of the world to come?'

As to the timing of history's curtain call, it remains a mystery—the only occasion on which Jesus confessed ignorance was in relation to his return (Matthew 24:36).

So Clinton, Castro and Gates will not receive a seven-day warning—but nor will anyone else. And whether that comes as a comfort or a challenge, it certainly serves as a deadline.

For further reading

PSALM 130:1–8

There are some men and women who can rightly expect to go down in history. Some of them live with one eye on how posterity will view them. But with the prospect of Jesus' second coming before us, we are reminded that neither greatness nor fame in this life are ultimately that important. Deuteronomy 34:12 says of Moses, 'No one has ever shown the mighty power... that Moses did.' Despite this, Numbers 12:3 says that 'Moses was a very humble man, more humble than anyone else on the face of the earth.' Moses' priority was not popularity and prestige but obedience to God. However 'successful' our lives appear, they will be judged as failures if we focus on ourselves and miss the challenge to be ready for the second coming of the Saviour of the world.

Prayer

When I survey the wondrous cross,
On which the Prince of glory died,
My richest gain I count but loss,
And pour contempt on all my pride.
ISAAC WATTS (1674–1748)

Welcome home!

'Be careful not to do your "acts of righteousness" before men, to be seen by them. If you do, you will have no reward from your Father in heaven.'

MATTHEW 6:1

Let's face it, we all like to be appreciated.

It doesn't have to be a bunch of flowers or an elaborate speech; for most of us, a simple 'thank you' will do. But that is where a conflict arises within most of us. After all, according to Jesus, our giving (and that surely includes acts of service) should be done so that the left hand doesn't see what the right hand is doing (Matthew 6:3).

So how come most of us want to be thanked, when we are meant to be doing it unnoticed? I suppose that is where we see our real motives in their stark and uncomfortable light. True goodness seeks no reward or recognition.

In the Sermon on the Mount, Jesus urges his followers to seek God's approval more than human applause. God sees what is done in secret and has his own methods of recognizing costly acts of love.

Some years ago, a missionary returned to the United States after thirty years of service for God in Africa. This was the era before people criss-crossed the globe in jet airliners, so he faced a long sea voyage to New York. On board the liner was the US President returning from a safari vacation.

As the ship docked, the quay was lined with thousands of spectators eager to welcome the President. There was a military band decked out in full regalia, plus a crowd of dignitaries lined up to shake the great man's hand. In true American style, the President drove away in an open-topped limousine with a shower of ticker tape cascading from the sky, as the crowd cheered enthusiastically.

After the fuss died away, the missionary made his way down the gangplank alone. No one had come to meet him. No helping hands to carry his luggage, no word of welcome. As he struggled along the quay, he felt overwhelmed with self-pity. 'Why, Lord?' he muttered under his breath. 'The President takes a vacation and they roll out the red carpet for him. I spent my life working for you and no one can be bothered to turn out and greet me. Aren't I worth a "welcome home"?'

An inner voice stopped him dead in his tracks. And he lived with the message to his dying day.

The voice spoke a sentence that melted his hard heart. 'You're not home yet,' it said.

For further reading

2 THESSALONIANS 1:1–12

Paul was a great encourager, spurring on the recipients of his letters to greater acts of service to God. It is hurtful to feel unappreciated or taken for granted. Encouragement helps us to keep going when we'd like to give up. Unfortunately it's not automatic or in direct proportion to our efforts. We have no control over it, and if we only do things in order to be seen and appreciated by other people it's likely to backfire on us. What we can do, however, is to be appreciative and encouraging ourselves. We can get into the habit of noticing what other people are doing and when they need a bit of sincere encouragement to keep them going. When we feel discouraged and tempted to give up, let us remind ourselves of Paul's words to the Galatians: 'Let us not become weary in doing good, for at the proper time we will reap a harvest if we do not give up' (6:9).

Prayer

Ask God to show you if there is someone in your church who needs to be encouraged in their service for him, then do it.

If you feel that you are working hard and being taken for granted—or worse, being criticized despite your efforts—thank God that he sees and that he knows your motives and that he will reward you. Remember, you're not home yet.

The foundation stone of a healthy life

For God so loved the world that he gave his one and only Son, that whoever believes in him shall not perish but have eternal life.
JOHN 3:16

I lost a friend this week. I use the word 'lost' in its temporary sense as I have no doubt we shall meet again soon. He had known for several months that he was terminally ill. Rarely have I seen anyone respond to this news in the way he did.

He carefully organized his affairs down to the last detail, making certain that everyone who needed to knew where to find things. The day before he died, we spent time chatting about a range of subjects. Before I left him, the conversation turned to heaven. Nothing unusual about that because, in the years I have known him, it often has.

The truth is, he had had his bags packed for months and was ready to make the journey. To me—and to those who knew him well—he was an eloquent example of what is described in the New Testament as 'living hope'. Peter, the Christian leader, expresses it well when he speaks of God's gift: 'In his great mercy he has given us new birth into a living hope through the resurrection of Jesus Christ from the dead' (1 Peter 1:3).

One of my abiding memories of my friend will be the way in which, through the last months of his life, he preached a sermon on that verse. In God's book, he died well.

Leonardo da Vinci, at the end of his life, reflected, 'While I thought I was learning to live, I have been learning how to die.'

It used to be that sex was the forbidden subject but now that honour, it seems, has been passed to death. That is foolishness, because learning to come to terms with our finite nature and what lies beyond is a foundation stone for healthy living.

A few weeks ago, I shared a train journey with a businessman. After the usual British pleasantries, he asked me what I did for a living. I told him and he looked stunned. 'Surely you don't believe all that stuff, do you?' His question was not meant to be rude and, having met some clerics who look and sound decidedly confused, I couldn't blame him for asking.

'Yes, I do,' I replied quietly.

If I had met him again this week following my friend's promotion to heaven, I'd have given the same answer.

Only louder. Much louder.

For further reading

REVELATION 19:1–9; HEBREWS 12:22–29

If we know Jesus as our Saviour, then we can know for certain that we have eternal life, that we won't cease to exist when our physical bodies die but will go to heaven to be with God eternally. With our imperfect, sinful minds, it's not possible for us to envisage fully what heaven will be like, although the Bible gives us glimpses of it. What we know now will pass away and be replaced by 'a kingdom that cannot be shaken' (Hebrews 12:28). All the uncertainties, sickness and sadness of this life will be over for us for all eternity. Not surprisingly, heaven won't be a quiet place; there will be exuberant, noisy rejoicing, with 'thousands upon thousands of angels' together with all those, like us, who have put their trust in Jesus (Hebrews 12:22–23). For the Christian, death is not the end but a doorway to something infinitely better than anything we have ever known.

Prayer

Hallelujah!
For our Lord God Almighty reigns.
Let us rejoice and be glad
and give him glory!
REVELATION 19:6–7

Acknowledgments

We would like to thank all those who have given us permission to include quotations in this book, as indicated in the list below. Every effort has been made to trace and contact copyright holders of all the quotations included. We apologize for any errors or omissions that may remain, and would ask those concerned to contact the publishers, who will ensure that full acknowledgment is made in the future.

Extract from 'Prayer of St Francis' dedicated to Mrs Frances Tracy. © 1967, OCP Publications, 5536 NE Hassalo, Portland OR 97213. All rights reserved. Used with permission.

'How deep the Father's love for us' by Stuart Townend, copyright © 1995 Kingsway's Thankyou Music, PO Box 75, Eastbourne, East Sussex, BN23 6NW, UK. Used by permission.

'Poor' by Steve Turner, from *The King of Twist*. Reproduced by permission of Hodder and Stoughton Limited.